TRADE
UNIONS

in the epoch of imperialist decay

TRADE UNIONS

in the epoch of imperialist decay

by Leon Trotsky

PREFACE BY FARRELL DOBBS

Trade Unions: their past, present, and future

by Karl Marx

PATHFINDER

New York London Montreal Sydney

Edited by John Riddell

ISBN 0-87348-583-1
Library of Congress Catalog Card Number 90-70744
Manufactured in Canada

First edition, 1990
Third printing, 2004

Cover design: Eva Braiman

Pathfinder

www.pathfinderpress.com
E-mail: pathfinderpress@compuserve.com

PATHFINDER DISTRIBUTORS AROUND THE WORLD:
Australia (and Southeast Asia and the Pacific):
    Pathfinder, Level 1, 3/281-287 Beamish St., Campsie, NSW 2194
    Postal address: P.O. Box 164, Campsie, NSW 2194
Canada:
    Pathfinder, 699 Lansdowne Ave., Toronto, ON M6H 3Y9
Iceland:
    Pathfinder, Skolavordustig 6B, Reykjavík
    Postal address: P. Box 0233, IS 121 Reykjavík
New Zealand:
    Pathfinder, P.O. Box 3025, Auckland
Sweden:
    Pathfinder, Domargränd 16, S-129 47 Hägersten
United Kingdom (and Europe, Africa, Middle East, and South Asia):
    Pathfinder, 47 The Cut, London, SE1 8LF
United States (and Caribbean, Latin America, and East Asia):
    Pathfinder Books, 306 W. 37th St., 10th Floor, New York, NY 10018-2852

Contents

Top: Karl Marx, 1872. Bottom: Farrell Dobbs (left) and Leon Trotsky in Mexico (1940).

About the authors

Leon Trotsky (1879–1940) was a central leader of the Russian revolution, the Communist Party of Russia, and the Communist International. During World War I he spent nearly two years in exile in France, where he worked with revolutionary syndicalist leaders such as Alfred Rosmer and Pierre Monatte. In the Soviet government of Russia that was brought to power by the workers and peasants in November 1917, Trotsky was commissar of foreign affairs and then commissar of war, leading the organization of the Red Army in the civil war of 1918–20. As a member of the Executive Committee of the Communist International (Comintern), Trotsky bore special responsibility for collaboration with revolutionaries in France.

In 1923 Trotsky and others began a fight to defend a Leninist course against the faction based on the growing bureaucracy in the Soviet government and Communist Party apparatus, whose foremost representative was Joseph Stalin. Trotsky was expelled from the Communist Party in 1927, removed from Moscow to the isolated town of Alma Ata in 1928, and forcibly exiled to Turkey in February 1929. He found asylum in France from July 1933 to mid-1935, in Norway until the end of 1936, and thereafter in Mexico.

In 1930 Trotsky organized the International Left Opposition to defend the Comintern from Stalinist degeneration. In 1933 he called for a break from the Stalinized Comintern and launched a fight for a new International, which led to the foundation of the Fourth International in 1938.

Leon Trotsky was assassinated in 1940 in Mexico by an agent of Stalin.

Karl Marx (1818–1883), together with Frederick Engels, was a founding leader of the international revolutionary workers' movement.

In 1847–51 he and Engels led the Communist League, an international association of revolutionary workers. In 1847–48 they wrote the Communist Manifesto as its program. During the revolution that swept Europe in 1848, Marx edited the Cologne daily *Neue Rheinische Zeitung*, which organized the revolutionary democratic forces in Germany. Following the defeat of the 1848 revolution, Marx was forced into exile in London.

In 1864 Marx participated in the establishment of the International Working Men's Association. He became a central leader of its General Council, devoting much of his time to the organization of international workers' solidarity.

In March 1871 a revolutionary government was established in Paris—the Commune. Marx's writings spearheaded the international campaign to defend the Paris Commune and explained its character as the first revolutionary government of the working people.

In 1867 Marx published the first volume of *Capital*, his analysis of the origins and inner workings of the capitalist economy and society, and of how its development prepares the ground for proletarian revolution. The second and third volumes, which he left incomplete, were published by Engels in 1885 and 1894.

Farrell Dobbs (1907–1983) joined the Communist League of America as a militant Teamsters leader during the historic 1934 Minneapolis trucking strikes, which were led by CLA members. These strikes showed the way in the battle that built powerful industrial unions in the United States in the 1930s.

Dobbs was the outstanding leader of the great battles that built a militant Teamsters union in Minnesota and neighboring states. He led the first campaign to unionize over-the-road truck drivers, which swept through eleven states in 1938. In 1940 he resigned from the union staff to become labor secretary of the Socialist Workers Party. Along with seventeen other SWP and Teamsters leaders, he was jailed during World War II under the notorious Smith Act for his communist views and his opposition to the imperialist war.

From 1953 to 1972 Dobbs was national secretary of the Socialist Workers Party. He was its presidential candidate four times between 1948 and 1960. He helped lead the participation of revolutionary socialists in the rising struggles of Black people and in defense of the Cuban and Vietnamese revolutions.

Dobbs authored a four-volume series *(Teamster Rebellion, Teamster Power, Teamster Politics,* and *Teamster Bureaucracy)* chronicling the development of revolutionary leadership in the 1934 strikes and the subsequent eight years of Teamsters union struggles. He is also the author of *Revolutionary Continuity: The Early Years 1848–1917* and *Revolutionary Continuity: Birth of the Communist Movement 1918–1922,* which recount the development of working-class leadership in the United States.

Introduction

The articles in this collection explain the fundamental dynamics of trade unions, which have served, since the onset of the industrial revolution two centuries ago, as the elementary organizations for defense of workers' conditions and rights. At the same time, these articles outline the necessary link between trade union organization and workers' fight for economic justice and political power—their fight to rid the world of capitalist exploitation and imperialist oppression.

Although written many years ago, these articles by Karl Marx and Leon Trotsky—two of the outstanding revolutionary leaders of the international workers' movement—have more than withstood the test of time; they are even more relevant today than when they were first written. The reader will repeatedly experience the shock of recognition at the descriptions in these pages of what happens to unions when they are improperly led and how badly they need to be transformed in order to be effective.

As this book is being published, at the opening of the 1990s, a capitalist earthquake is ravaging the semicolonial countries, precipitated by the massive external debt crisis. In Eastern and Central Europe and the Soviet Union, workers are beginning to resist imposition of the depression-like conditions that millions are sure lie in store for them. In the strongest capitalist

[NOTES TO THE INTRODUCTION ARE FOUND ON P. 29.]

countries of North America, Europe, Asia, and the Pacific, ominous tremors—from the massive corporate debt balloon, to instability of the banking system, to the employers' unabated offensive against workers and the unions—point to a coming economic and social crisis. This crisis will engulf working people the world over, producing mass unemployment, homelessness, and mounting pauperization.

The crisis conditions ahead will generate further struggles and revolts by workers acting to defend themselves and other exploited producers from capitalism's devastating effects. Routine "labor relations" will be swept aside by mounting class struggles. Workers will seek to use the trade unions as weapons to fight against wage cuts and attacks on health and safety; for jobs, a shorter workweek, and affirmative action; against dirty and devastating wars and the crushing economic and social burdens thrust upon colonial and semicolonial countries by the world's richest capitalist powers. Unorganized workers in their millions will once again reach toward the union movement. The employers will redouble attempts to weaken the unions and, where possible, to smash them.

Central to the outcome of these mighty class battles will be the struggle to transform the trade unions into revolutionary instruments that are part of the broader political fight by the working class to replace rule by the exploiters with governments of workers and working farmers. Thus, the employer-led onslaught against labor will increasingly include far-reaching assaults on democratic rights and on the space for working people to organize and practice politics, as the ruling capitalist families fight to preserve not only their profits and prerogatives but also their state power.

Rank-and-file militants in strikes and other union fights already taking place at the opening of the 1990s will find these articles by Karl Marx and Leon Trotsky particularly useful to read and study. The lessons contained in them, based on experiences of the workers' movement over the past 150 years, are not only part of the necessary preparation for the conditions and battles that lie ahead, they will also make us more effective unionists and political activists today.

❋

"Trade Unions: Their Past, Present, and Future" by Karl Marx has been an invaluable guide for union fighters ever since it was written in 1866. It has not been easily accessible, however. Reprinted as the prologue to the present collection, this document was originally a resolution to guide the trade union work of members of the International Working Men's Association, better known as the First International. Marx was the central leader of the association from its founding in London in 1864, under the impetus of a wave of working-class struggles that had been building since the late 1850s.

The significance of the First International is explained by Farrell Dobbs in his book *Revolutionary Continuity: The Early Years: 1848–1917*. Dobbs is also the author of the prefaces in this collection to the two sections containing articles by Leon Trotsky.

Marx and other leaders of the First International, Dobbs explains, recognized that the task of emancipating the working class "was not limited to either local or national perspectives, but embraced all countries. The working class needed not only its own domestic social policy but its own internationalist foreign policy. The International organized rallies and demonstrations in solidarity with the Polish struggle for national independence, as well as freedom of Ireland from British rule. It championed the war to defeat the Confederacy in the United States, projecting the need to transform it into a revolutionary war to emancipate the slaves and crush the slaveholding system and planter class."

The activity of the International Working Men's Association, Dobbs says, "soon began to stimulate trade union organization generally. International campaigns to back major strikes in one or another country helped to raise the workers' sights beyond national horizons. Support of demands for progressive labor legislation provided a way to introduce more advanced political ideas into the trade unions, especially the need to form independent parties of the working class."[1] The resolution drafted by Marx and adopted by the International's 1866 congress in Geneva, Switzerland, provided an orientation for this trade union work.

"Trade Unions: Their Past, Present, and Future" later served as one of the guides used by V.I. Lenin in building the Bolshevik Party, which led the workers and peasants to power in Russia in the October revolution of 1917. "The resolution," Lenin wrote in 1899, "recognised that the trade unions were not only a natural, but also an essential phenomenon under capitalism and considered them an extremely important means for organising the working class in its daily struggle against capital and for the abolition of wage-labour." The resolution underlined that the unions "must not remain aloof from the general political and social movement of the working class," Lenin said, but "must strive for the general emancipation of the millions of oppressed workers." The conviction central to the resolution "that the class struggle must necessarily combine the political and the economic struggle into one integral whole has entered into the flesh and blood" of the world revolutionary workers' movement, Lenin concluded.[2]

※

Marx's starting point for discussing the trade unions was the division of capitalist society into conflicting social classes with irreconcilable interests. An individual worker acting alone against the employer is powerless, Marx explained. That accounts for how trade unions are born, why they are necessary, and why they will continue to appear as long as capitalism exists.

By 1866 the unions were already suffering from their isolation from broader social and political struggles by working people. The existing unions tended to be organized and divided along craft lines. As a result, only a thin layer of workers was organized, leaving the big majority, including most of those in large factories, without any union protection.

Marx's comments on the future of the trade unions are especially relevant for the challenges facing the labor movement in the years ahead. More than 125 years after Marx wrote that the unions "cannot fail to enlist the nonsociety [unorganized] men into their ranks," for example, a large and growing majority of workers in the United States have not been organized into the union movement.

Marx singles out farm laborers as a section of the working class who are the "worst-paid" because they have been "rendered powerless by exceptional circumstances." To this day, the unions have by and large defaulted on organizing and championing the interests of millions of farm workers. These workers usually have no steady employment, receive among the lowest wages for working long hours at difficult and dangerous field work, and are subjected to unsanitary and humiliating living conditions in migrant camps. Farm workers are a bridge between the unions and all rural producers, including working farmers. Drawing agricultural laborers into a fighting union movement is indispensable to building an alliance of workers and farmers.

In the United States, Western Europe, and industrialized capitalist countries elsewhere, the challenge of organizing farm workers and other workers now outside the unions is closely linked to the task of organizing the growing numbers of immigrant workers, many of whom are from Third World countries.

Marx emphasizes that unions must convince "the world at large that their efforts, far from being narrow and selfish, aim at the emancipation of the downtrodden millions." In today's world, the unions should be organizing and taking the leadership of an international fight against the worsening imperialist plunder of the oppressed countries of Africa, Asia, Latin America, and the Pacific. At the close of the 1980s, the foreign debt foisted on these countries by the bankers of the United States, Canada, Japan, Western Europe, Australia, and New Zealand approached a staggering $1.5 trillion. The human toll of this massive debt burden is becoming ever more unbearable.

✳

The title piece in this collection, "Trade Unions in the Epoch of Imperialist Decay," was written in 1940 by Leon Trotsky, a central leader of the October 1917 revolution in Russia who had been forced into exile by Joseph Stalin in 1929. Trotsky examines the challenges before the trade unions in the imperialist era, in which capitalism has become a crisis-ridden world system marked by economic and social convulsions, wars, national liberation struggles, and intensifying battles by workers and farmers.

Trotsky notes a "degeneration of modern trade union organizations throughout the world" in terms of their capacity to defend workers' interests. The "common feature" in this development, he adds, "is their drawing close to and growing together with the state power" of the ruling capitalist classes.

In assessing this weakening of union power, Trotsky grounded himself in Lenin's explanation of how in the imperialist countries a narrow layer of privileged workers has emerged that mistakenly believes it has a stake in the capitalist order and thus often acts against the interests of the working class as a whole. The widespread development of this "aristocracy of labor" was made possible by the growth of imperialism into a world system toward the end of the nineteenth century. The superprofits drawn by the capitalists from their monopoly practices and exploitation of colonial and semicolonial countries allow them to grant concessions to a better-off layer of workers in the imperialist countries. The corruption of this layer provides a base of support for the policies of the union officialdom, who strive to collaborate with the employing class and display a chauvinist loyalty toward "their" national states. The entire working class and labor movement are increasingly weakened by these class-collaborationist policies.[3]

＊

In 1940, as Trotsky drafted "Trade Unions in the Epoch of Imperialist Decay," the interimperialist slaughter known as World War II had broken out and was dragging ever greater portions of the globe into the maelstrom. Throughout the 1930s, capitalism had been battered by a sweeping and cataclysmic depression and social crisis, signaled by the October 1929 Wall Street stock market crash.

Over the course of that decade, massive working-class struggles in the United States and several other countries had succeeded in forging industrial unions—that is, unions embracing all workers in a particular industry, not just the much smaller numbers in each of the various crafts. In France and Spain revolutionary crises had erupted, opening the possibility for workers and farmers to establish their own governments. The working-class movement, however, failed to carve out a revolutionary leadership that could lead workers and farmers in a struggle for power. The misleadership of the Stalinist-dominated Communist parties, together with that of their Social Democratic counterparts, organized the defeat of this workers' upsurge. Fascism, already used successfully in Italy in the early 1920s as a method of last resort to maintain capitalist rule, carried out the same task in Germany, Spain, and other European countries, crushing workers' organizations.

Developments in the U.S. labor movement at this time illustrate some of the main trends Trotsky identified in his 1940 article, trends that in the post–World War II period led to further setbacks to the labor movement. By the mid-1930s a vast social movement of working people was on the rise in the United States. The trade unions moved to the center stage of U.S. politics, with the Congress of Industrial Organizations (CIO) at the forefront. By the end of the decade the percentage of the

U.S. working class that was unionized had jumped from 5 percent to close to 16 percent. The battles that forged the CIO also marked a big step forward against racial segregation, including in the labor movement, since the new industrial unions organized all workers in a given factory, regardless of race. Black workers by the tens of thousands moved into the front ranks as fighting leaders of union struggles.

By the latter half of 1937, however, the momentum of the CIO's rise was already slowing down. Important strikes in auto, coal, and steel over the next few years were largely rearguard actions. Bureaucratic control of the newly established industrial unions was starting to be exerted. Preparations for U.S. entry into the war were increasingly being used by Pres. Franklin Roosevelt to justify restrictions on democratic and labor rights.

The Communist Party, many of whose members held major leadership posts in the industrial unions, joined with other top officials in pursuing class-collaborationist policies; they subordinated working-class interests to cementing a place for the CIO officialdom in the Roosevelt-led Democratic Party coalition. This Stalinist course was decisive in derailing the evolution of the CIO as a social movement. Union leadership of a deepening fight against racial segregation and divisions in the working class was set back, as well. The road was blocked to using union power to advance independent labor political action and the fight for a workers' and farmers' government.

The outstanding revolutionary workers' leader to emerge from the U.S. labor radicalization of the 1930s was Farrell Dobbs. A young worker in an unorganized coal yard, Dobbs joined Minneapolis Teamsters Local 574 (later 544) and helped lead three strikes in 1934 that won union recognition and a contract for truckers and related workers in that city. He became the central figure in the class-struggle leadership of the Teamsters based in Minneapolis and extending across Minnesota and various other states in the Midwest.

The Minneapolis Teamsters leadership set an example for the entire labor movement by organizing the membership to make decisions and act to advance the interests of workers and farmers, independent of the needs of the employers, their government, and their political parties. The Teamsters leaders advocated formation of a labor party based on the unions, defended colonial freedom struggles, and championed the fight for equality by Blacks and other oppressed nationalities. These leaders fought every move by government agencies to bring the labor movement to heel and thus to gut union power.

What most set the Minneapolis Teamsters leaders apart from those in the top U.S. labor officialdom, however, was their outspoken opposition to the Roosevelt administration's headlong preparations to join in the spreading interimperialist war. It was for this reason that Roosevelt's Justice Department in 1941 handed down indictments on charges of "sedition" against the Teamsters leaders, as well as several leaders of the Socialist Workers Party. (The International officialdom of the Teamsters cooperated in the government's assault.) These prosecutions were Washington's first use of the Smith "gag" Act, adopted the previous year, which turned the mere expression of ideas into grounds for imprisonment. Dobbs and seventeen others were found guilty of sedition and put in prison.[4]

Other federal prosecutions soon followed. In 1942 sedition indictments were brought against sixty-three members of the Temple of Islam (later renamed the Nation of Islam), including its leader Elijah Muhammad. Their "crime" was refusing to accept the racist, anti-Japanese stereotypes that were a major part of U.S. war propaganda. This was one of many episodes in the government's efforts during the war to counter the growing Black rights fight.

With the overwhelming bulk of the top labor officialdom putting up no opposition, the U.S capitalist rulers were unhindered in dragging workers and farmers into the bloodbath of World War II in December 1941. The labor bureaucracy in its big majority fell in step with Roosevelt's war policies, insisting that the interests of union members and other working people had to be subordinated to "national unity." The unions were drawn more tightly than ever into cooperation with the capitalist state, as the officialdom assumed direct responsibility for enforcing longer hours, speedup, wage freezes, a no-strike pledge, and otherwise policing the workers on behalf of the employing class. Union officials who were cadres of the Stalinist Communist Party earned the hatred of struggle-minded workers for their special zeal in these efforts to cram austerity and labor discipline down the throats of the working class.

*

Part 2 of this collection consists of articles by Trotsky directed toward radicalizing worker militants who were attracted to syndicalism. The syndicalists, or anarcho-syndicalists, were a radical current in the labor movement in the first decades of this century. They sought to overthrow capitalist exploitation through the direct action of industrial trade unions alone, direct action they assumed would reach its climax in a revolutionary general strike.

Like the anarchists, to whom they were closely related, syndicalists rejected all "politics," including participation in political parties of any kind. They denied the need for any form of workers' government or state in the transition to socialism following a revolutionary triumph. The syndicalists claimed to keep the unions out of "politics." The problem is that "politics" does not ignore the unions. Despite the revolutionary convictions of many syndicalist fighters, their course obstructed the development of a communist party needed by the working class to take on the capitalist state and political parties. Syndicalism also posed an obstacle to the development of effective industrial unions, which seek to draw in the broadest layers of workers, regardless of current political affiliation.

Following the October 1917 revolution in Russia, many revolutionary-minded syndicalists were won to the Communist International and its parties. Some, however, while cooperating with communists to varying degrees on the trade union level, held aloof from the communist movement itself, denying that workers should attempt to build an international organization of revolutionary political parties. In discussions with these syndicalists, Trotsky's views were therefore rooted in the principles explained by Marx—the need for trade unions to place themselves in the forefront of broad social and political struggles and not to limit themselves to so-called trade union issues. It is these lessons that make these articles so relevant today, at a time when revolutionary syndicalism is no longer, and is not likely to become, a major factor in the working-class movement.

＊

At the opening of the 1990s, the trade unions in the United States are weaker than at any time since the rise of the CIO more than a half century ago. Here as in other imperialist countries, workers and their unions are hamstrung by class-collaborationist institutions and policies extending from shop floor cooperation with the bosses to support for the national interests and state apparatus of the ruling class in each country. This pattern of "stable labor-management cooperation" enforced by an entrenched bureaucracy began to take shape in the United States in the preparations for World War II and was accentuated during the war itself. The pattern was consolidated during the initial period of political reaction and Cold War in the late 1940s and early 1950s. With the willing assistance of the labor bureaucracy, the government succeeded in wrapping the unions in layers of red tape that have fettered the ranks from exercising union power to defend their interests ever since.

Following the sharp worldwide capitalist recession of 1974–75, the employing class in the imperialist countries launched a sustained offensive against the working class and the unions, aimed at transforming the unions into fully obedient servants of the drive for corporate profits. The rulers also began tightening their squeeze on peasants and workers in colonial and semicolonial countries.

In the wake of the 1981–82 recession, the retreat of the labor movement under the blows of the employers' offensive turned into an all-out rout of the unions in the United States. As the union officialdom capitulated to the bosses' demands, workers saw no perspective for successful resistance and began running away from the fight. Union members went along with, and often voted for, not only cuts in wages, concessions on job safety, and speedup, but also multitiered wage scales and the introduction of part-time- and temporary-worker schemes that deepened divisions in the work force and in the union. The lack of resistance was such that the employers, in general, had no need for direct government intervention on their behalf.

In the face of this employer offensive, the class-collaborationist course of the AFL-CIO officialdom has deepened, focusing in more than ever on how to keep "our" company and "our" industry "well managed" and profitable. Increasingly the policies pursued by the bureaucrats have gone in the direction of somehow becoming junior partners of the bosses, somehow getting a share in the prerogatives of capital.

In "Trade Unions in the Epoch of Imperialist Decay," Trotsky spoke of how the reformist bureaucracy of the unions acted as a "petty but active stockholder" of capitalist enterprises. He meant this as a metaphor to describe the bureaucracy's increasing role as a direct agent of the employing class. But the insight of metaphor has become the literal truth today, as the officials push schemes for the unions to sink pension funds and other resources of the membership into stocks and massive debt holdings and to negotiate so-called Employee Stock Ownership Plans. The bureaucrats increasingly seek ways to ensure that they have a say over selecting "good" management, and that union officials be given spots on boards of directors, creditors' committees, and so on. A greater percentage than ever of union treasuries is being spent not only on lawyers and consultants, but for the "services" of financial advisers, investment banking counselors, and corporate takeover specialists. In the United States, this has become a substantially bigger drain on union resources than even the long-standing expenditures on Washington lobbyists and "political action committees" to help elect "friendly" Democratic and Republican party candidates. This course of ever more deeply identifying the interests of workers and the bosses—of trying to yoke the union and the board of directors to the same plow—further undermines the use of union power, reinforcing the class-collaborationist policies that have increasingly weakened the labor movement for more than half a century. Contracts are negotiated with termination dates pushed further and further into the future. Contracts become longer and ever more complicated legal documents that serve as operations manuals for management, rather than as a clear guide to workers of the rights, wages, and conditions they have won at a particular point in their ongoing struggle with the boss.

The differential in pay and job conditions widens among workers doing the same job side by side in union shops. Next to nothing is done to lead campaigns to organize the growing number of nonunion factories, mines, mills, and other workplaces. Instead of using the power of the labor movement to lead a political fight for federally funded social programs to meet the needs of the entire class and other working people, the bureaucrats continue to deepen reliance on negotiated company-by-company health and pension plans for which workers are pressed to pay a growing share. And the officialdom continues to subordinate the unions to capitalist—usually Democratic Party—politicians. Yet as the framework of capitalist politics shifts to the right, these politicians pay less heed than ever before to the bureaucracy's wish list of labor and social legislation.

The fruit of this evolution, of this complete break in continuity with the labor upsurge of the mid-1930s, is that the unions that originated in the CIO function less like industrial unions—even in a limited trade union sense—than ever before in their history. The growing acceptance of multitiered wage structures, contract labor with little or no union protection, and similar schemes reinforce aristocratic and reactionary social attitudes among better-off layers in the labor movement; it heads back in the direction of the inequalities and divisions among workers characteristic of craft unionism.

＊

Despite more than a decade of the employers' antilabor offensive and the continued rotting out of the unions under their current misleadership, the U.S. and other imperialist ruling classes have nonetheless failed to accomplish what they must do to lay the basis for a sustained period of capitalist expansion and social and political stability. They have not reversed their declining rate of profit. And they have not broken the resistance of the working class to the degree necessary to fundamentally alter the relationship of forces between labor and capital. Thus, the decisive battles between the capitalists and the workers still lie ahead.

Decades of bureaucratization of the industrial unions have shaped the conditions in which these working-class struggles will begin to unfold. When Trotsky wrote "Trade Unions in the Epoch of Imperialist Decay"—in the aftermath of a powerful labor upsurge—the capitalists had to draw the bureaucracy more tightly into the apparatus of the state in order to quell working-class resistance and crush class struggle–minded currents. By the 1980s, however, the officialdom had largely succeeded in driving the ranks out of active participation in the unions.

The experience of coal miners in the United States over the past two decades confirms that workers—as they come into sharper confrontation with the employers—are propelled toward taking back their unions, so they can bring union power to bear to win the fights they are forced into. At the end of the 1960s the ranks of the United Mine Workers of America (UMWA) began to confront the decline of their union. Coal miners launched a militant movement of strikes and mass mobilizations around vital issues of health and safety. In trying to bring the union's power into this struggle against the coal operators and the government, miners ran up against the corrupt UMWA bureaucracy, led by Tony Boyle, which resorted to hooliganism and cold-blooded murder to subdue the ranks. But Boyle's gang was beaten back by the miners and ousted from the leadership by the rank-and-file Miners for Democracy movement. (Boyle himself was convicted of murder and imprisoned.) The ranks carved out space for the union democracy they needed to marshal their strength against the coal operators. Miners waged successful strike battles in 1977–78 and 1981; coal operators backed off from confrontations with the union when contracts came up in 1984 and again in 1988. At the end of the 1980s the UMWA, alone among major industrial unions in the United States, had been able to hold off concessions of the scope and character that marked the rout of the labor movement earlier in the decade.

What took place in the UMWA in the late 1960s and early 1970s was nothing less than a revolution by the miners to win effective control of their union, sufficient to deploy union power against the coal operators. The momentum of this victory accounts for the continuing relative strength and combativity of the UMWA. For other unions that crossroads still lies ahead. But each of them will approach it, and sooner than many think.

✳

In the latter half of the 1980s, layers of workers in the United States began to put up growing resistance to efforts by capitalists in some industries to press the union movement harder and deepen the union-busting pattern of the previous several years. Strike battles have been waged by packinghouse workers, paperworkers, coal miners, airline workers, and others. Workers such as these are blazing a trail to be emulated by others of not cowing before the bosses' takeback demands, of putting up a fight, of reaching out for unity and solidarity of working people—both in North America and worldwide.

Over this same period, Wall Street experienced two stock market crashes (October 1987 and October 1989); the U.S. savings and loan system went into an accelerating decline; the massive Third World debt crisis plunged a number of semicolonial countries into the worst depression conditions since the 1930s; corporate debt mushroomed to destabilizing heights in the United States; interimperialist economic competition stiffened sharply; and capitalist investment in new plant and equipment continued to stagnate. All these conditions underline the international capitalist system's growing vulnerability to a banking collapse in the 1990s and point to the worldwide depression and social crisis such a collapse would inevitably open.

Militant working-class battles and an international labor radicalization are on the agenda in the closing decade of the twentieth century. The working class enters this period having suffered no major defeats, such as the triumph of fascism in Germany in the early 1930s. Moreover, the world Stalinist movement will not dominate the politicized workers' movement as it did half a century ago; it is in a much weaker position to block the development of mass revolutionary currents in the unions.

In addition, the coming labor radicalization will build on the conquests of social struggles in the 1960s and early 1970s and their impact on the conditions and consciousness of the working class and labor movement. The fight for Black rights, women's rights, immigrants' rights, opposition to imperialist war, support for the rights of lesbians and gays and of the disabled, opposition to nuclear power and environmental degradation—all these have deeply affected the trade unions and will continue to do so.

At some point in the evolution of the coming labor struggles—as more battles take place and fortify each other, as a growing percentage of union and unorganized workers get involved in struggle, as reinforcement comes from fights by working farmers and social and political struggles outside the unions—the cumulative impact will begin to shatter the existing leadership structures of the labor movement. Larger and larger layers of workers will seek to transform the unions into instruments of revolutionary class struggle.

Such an explosive upsurge of labor battles will once again be met—as in the period of the last great labor radicalization, described by Trotsky—by efforts on the part of the bosses and labor bureaucracy to tie the unions more closely to the capitalist state as instruments to police and control the working class. Capitalist governments will step up the direct use of state power against the unions and against revolutionary currents in the labor movement. In such conditions, the class struggle will begin moving at unanticipated and accelerating speed. If vanguard fighters in the working class and unions wait for such developments to break over them before beginning to prepare for battle, it will be too late.

Out of the initial rounds of labor struggles that are already opening, rank-and-file leaders are being tested in action and gaining invaluable experience for the bigger class battles ahead. But fighting workers cannot be prepared for what is coming simply by trying to generalize lessons from the battles they are directly engaged in. They need to draw on the experience of broader layers of workers and farmers—not only from a particular region or country, but worldwide; not only from today, but from past struggles by working people.

Many important political and strategic guidelines for workers who are actively involved in union battles and other struggles are described in the reports and resolutions of the U.S. Socialist Workers Party collected in the Pathfinder book *The Changing Face of U.S. Politics: Building a Party of Socialist Workers.* Some central programmatic demands that the international labor movement needs to campaign for in the period we are entering are outlined in the 1988 SWP resolution *An Action Program to Confront the Coming Economic Crisis.* This document focuses on the need to unify the workers against the employers by fighting for a shorter workweek with no cut in pay to combat unemployment and provide jobs for all; for affirmative ac-

tion quotas aimed at advancing equality for Blacks, other oppressed nationalities, and women; and for cancellation of the
Third World debt to unite workers around the world against
the consequences of imperialist exploitation, which not only
perpetuate oppression in semicolonial countries but threaten
all working people with devastation from capitalist-caused de-
pressions, environmental destruction, and war.[5]

The publication of this collection of articles by Karl Marx
and Leon Trotsky is part of the necessary preparation of working-class fighters to forge a new kind of leadership of the labor
movement, as we move toward the mightiest class battles of
human history. These battles will provide workers and exploited
farmers the opportunity to conquer political power from the
exploiting minority and take another historic step forward in
the fight for a socialist world.

It is to provide another political weapon for the workers who
have already begun fighting today, and who in doing so are
strengthening our class for the battles we will fight tomorrow,
that this book is being published.

Joel Britton
Margaret Jayko
MAY 1990

*Joel Britton is an oil worker and a member of the Oil, Chemi-
cal and Atomic Workers union in Los Angeles, California. Margaret Jayko is a garment worker and a member of the International Ladies' Garment Workers' Union in San Francisco,
California.*

Notes

1. Farrell Dobbs, *Revolutionary Continuity: Marxist Leadership in the U.S.*, vol. 1, *The Early Years 1848–1917* (New York: Anchor Foundation, a Pathfinder book, 1980), pp. 28–30. The second of Dobbs's two volumes is subtitled *Birth of the Communist Movement 1918–1922* (New York: Anchor Foundation, a Pathfinder book, 1983).

2. V.I. Lenin, "A Protest by Russian Social-Democrats," in *Collected Works* (Moscow: Progress Publishers, 1960–71), vol. 4, pp. 176–77.

3. Trotsky differentiates between the role of the labor bureaucracy in imperialist countries and semicolonial countries. In the former it serves as a prop to help the ruling capitalist families perpetuate the world imperialist system. In the colonial countries the union officialdom is most often allied with sectors of the national capitalist class seeking a bigger slice of the pie from international monopoly capital.

4. Dobbs tells the story of the 1934 Minneapolis strikes, the subsequent organizing drives across the north-central states, the political evolution of the class-struggle leadership of Local 544, and the Smith Act prosecution in his four-volume series published by Pathfinder: *Teamster Rebellion, Teamster Power, Teamster Politics,* and *Teamster Bureaucracy.*

5. See Jack Barnes, ed., *The Changing Face of U.S. Politics: Building a Party of Socialist Workers* (New York: Pathfinder, 1981) and *An Action Program to Confront the Coming Economic Crisis* (New York: Pathfinder, 1989).

A note on sources

"Trade Unions: Their Past, Present, and Future," the prologue to this book, was written by Karl Marx in English for the 1866 Geneva congress of the International Working Men's Association. It was published in early 1867 in the association's journal, *International Courier,* and is taken from Karl Marx and Frederick Engels, *Collected Works* (New York: International Publishers, 1985), vol. 20, pp. 191–92.

Trotsky's "Letter to a French Syndicalist on the Communist Party," placed at the beginning of part 2, has long been inaccessible. It is taken from issue 13 of the English-language edition of the magazine *Communist International,* published in 1920, and has been revised after comparison with the German edition.

The other material in this book was published in 1969 by Pathfinder as *Leon Trotsky on the Trade Unions.* The sequence of Trotsky's articles has been altered from that in the 1969 book.

The two prefaces by Farrell Dobbs, also taken from *Leon Trotsky on the Trade Unions,* have been slightly altered to allow for the changes in the ordering of Trotsky's articles.

English-language versions of the articles in part 1 first appeared in the 1930s in the U.S. weekly, the *Militant,* and other periodicals associated with the struggle led by Trotsky to rebuild the international communist movement on the foundations laid by Lenin. With the exception of the 1920 letter, Trotsky's articles in part 2 first appeared in English in the pamphlet *Communism and Syndicalism,* published in 1931 by the Communist League of America.

The translations in the 1969 book have been used in this collection with only minor alterations. The texts have been checked and edited against available texts in Russian and other source languages. Further translation and annotation for this book was done by Bob Schwarz.

An index and expanded notes are included, as well as a glossary of names of individuals and organizations that may be unfamiliar to the reader.

John Riddell

French syndicalists and communists on trial for involvement in May 1920 strike movement. Seated in front row of dock, from left to right: Pierre Monatte, Boris Souvarine, Fernand Loriot, Gaston Monmousseau. They were acquitted March 17, 1921.

Top: Alfred Rosmer (left) with Trotsky in Trotsky's study in Mexico, 1939.
Bottom: French sit-down strike, 1936.

Union militants move to defend picket lines against police assault during one of 1934 strikes by Minneapolis Teamsters. Central organizer of union pickets in these strikes was Farrell Dobbs.

Sit-down strikers, members of newly organized United Auto Workers union, inside Ford assembly plant in Kansas City, 1937.

Prologue

Trade unions: their past, present, and future

by Karl Marx

The following resolution was adopted by the first congress of the International Working Men's Association (the First International), held September 1866 in Geneva, Switzerland. It was drafted in English by Marx as part of a set of guidelines for the delegates.

(A) THEIR PAST

Capital is concentrated social force, while the workman has only to dispose of his working force [labor power]. The *contract* between capital and labor can therefore never be struck on equitable terms, equitable even in the sense of a society which places the ownership of the material means of life and labor on one side and the vital productive energies on the opposite side. The only social power of the workmen is their number. The force of numbers, however, is broken by disunion. The disunion of the workmen is created and perpetuated by their *unavoidable competition among themselves.*

Trades' unions originally sprang up from the *spontaneous* attempts of workmen at removing or at least checking that competition, in order to conquer such terms of contract as might raise them at least above the condition of mere slaves. The immediate object of trades' unions was therefore confined to everyday necessities, to expediences for the obstruction of the incessant encroachments of capital, in one word, to questions of wages and time of labor. This activity of the trades' unions is not only legitimate, it is necessary. It cannot be dispensed with so long as the present system of production lasts. On the contrary, it must be generalized by the formation and the combination of trades' unions throughout all countries. On the other hand, unconsciously to themselves, the trades' unions were forming *centers of organization* of the working class, as the medieval municipalities and communes did for the middle class. If the trades' unions are required for the guerrilla fights between capital and labor, they are still more important as *organized agencies for superseding the very system of wages labor and capital rule.*

(B) THEIR PRESENT

Too exclusively bent upon the local and immediate struggles with capital, the trades' unions have not yet fully understood their power of acting against the system of wages slavery itself. They therefore kept too much aloof from general social and political movements. Of late, however, they seem to awaken to some sense of their great historical mission, as appears, for instance, from their participation, in England, in the recent political movement, from the enlarged views taken of their function in the United States, and from the following resolution passed at the recent great conference of trades' delegates at Sheffield:[1]

"That this conference, fully appreciating the efforts made by the International [Working Men's] Association to unite in one common bond of brotherhood the working men of all countries, most earnestly recommend to the various societies here represented, the advisability of becoming affiliated to that body, believing that it is essential to the progress and prosperity of the entire working community."

(c) THEIR FUTURE

Apart from their original purposes, they must now learn to act deliberately as organizing centers of the working class in the broad interest of its *complete emancipation*. They must aid every social and political movement tending in that direction. Considering themselves and acting as the champions and representatives of the whole working class, they cannot fail to enlist the nonsociety [unorganized] men into their ranks. They must look carefully after the interests of the worst-paid trades, such as the agricultural laborers, rendered powerless by exceptional circumstances. They must convince the world at large that their efforts, far from being narrow and selfish, aim at the emancipation of the downtrodden millions.

Part 1

*Problems of trade union
strategy and tactics*

Preface

BY FARRELL DOBBS

As a Marxist, Leon Trotsky of course was deeply concerned with all the problems relating to the revolutionary mobilization of the working class, and he followed with interest changes in the trade unions of various countries and the problems of strategy and tactics that these changes presented for revolutionists. In fact at the time of his death in 1940 he was working on such questions in the piece "Trade Unions in the Epoch of Imperialist Decay."

This article, which is must reading for every Marxist, whether or not he is active in the unions, is one of the most brilliant and prophetic Trotsky ever wrote. Far-ranging, pointing to the conditions that were common to unions all over the world at the start of World War II, it penetrates to the central question of unionism in our time: the need for "complete and unconditional independence of the trade unions in relation to the capitalist state." It is indeed a pity that Trotsky did not live to complete this article, but there is more food for thought (and action) in this short unfinished piece than will be found in any book by anyone else on the union question.

The second article is about "The Question of Trade Union Unity" as it presented itself to the French Left Oppositionists in 1931, when the unions were divided into two rival labor federations. But Trotsky's treatment of this recurring problem transcends the particular situation that led him to write it and offers guidelines for handling it even today.

"We make no fetish of trade union unity," he wrote. "It is

not a question for us of a panacea." But at the same time, he stressed, "a preference for an assured majority in a narrow and isolated trade union confederation rather than oppositional work in a broad and real mass organization, is the mark only of sectarians or officials and not of proletarian revolutionists." He did not advocate trade union unity at all times and under all conditions, but he pointed out its advantages under most conditions for the working class as a whole and for the revolutionists in particular.

The third article, here entitled "The Unions in Britain," was written in 1933 after Hitler's coming to power had revealed the bankruptcy of the Communist International (Comintern). The Left Opposition had decided to discontinue its efforts to reform the Comintern and its parties and to work for the creation of a new International. In line with this, the Left Opposition participated in an international conference of left socialist and independent communist organizations held in Paris August 27–28, 1933, where it introduced a resolution advocating a new International. One of the centrist organizations at the conference, the Independent Labour Party of Great Britain, took an intermediate position on this question because it was still suffering from illusions about the possibility of reforming the Comintern—illusions that were partly the result of ignorance about the history of Stalinism.

In this article, written shortly after the Paris conference, Trotsky undertook the task of educating the members of the ILP not only about the disastrous policies of the Stalinists in the union sphere in Britain and elsewhere, but also about the role of genuine revolutionists in combating the union bureaucracy. Among other questions, he deals here with one that has still not died: Is it not possible to skip over the trade union stage?

The fourth article consists of excerpts from letters in 1936, 1937, and 1938 criticizing the Revolutionary Socialist Workers Party (RSAP) of Holland, which had adhered to the movement for a new International at the Paris conference in 1933, but which developed a number of serious differences in the following years and withdrew from the movement before the Fourth International was founded in 1938.

The differences covered a broad range of questions—the civil war in Spain, the nature and internal life of the Fourth International, and others. But they also concerned the RSAP's union policy, which was concentrated on a small independent grouping, the National Labor Secretariat (NAS), in which RSAP leader Henk Sneevliet played a leading role, but which remained outside of the mainstream of the Dutch labor movement.

The fifth article is taken from the main document adopted at the founding conference of the Fourth International, "The Death Agony of Capitalism and the Tasks of the Fourth International." It repeats the need for revolutionists to work inside the existing unions and condemns "sectarian attempts to build or preserve small 'revolutionary' unions" as "the renouncing of the struggle for leadership of the working class." But it also rejects "trade union fetishism, equally characteristic of trade unionists and syndicalists." It advocates a struggle not only to replace the conservative union bureaucracy but also to create wherever possible independent militant organizations better suited to mass anticapitalist struggle; and, if necessary, "not flinching even in the face of a direct break with the conservative apparatus of the trade unions. If it be criminal to turn one's back on mass organizations for the sake of fostering sectarian fictions, it is no less so to passively tolerate subordination of the revolutionary mass movement to the control of openly reactionary or disguised conservative ('progressive') bureaucratic cliques. Trade unions are not ends in themselves; they are but means along the road to proletarian revolution."

The final article in part 1 is the product of a conversation Trotsky had with a CIO organizer in Mexico in September 1938, shortly after the founding of the Fourth International.

Other writings and discussions by Trotsky on union problems, especially American problems, will be found in *The Transitional Program for Socialist Revolution,* published by Pathfinder Press.

1969

August 1940

Trade unions in the epoch of imperialist decay

This unfinished article was found in Trotsky's desk after his assassination in August 1940. It first appeared in *Fourth International*, February 1941.

There is one common feature in the development, or more correctly the degeneration, of modern trade union organizations throughout the world: it is their drawing close to and growing together with the state power. This process is equally characteristic of the neutral, the Social Democratic, the Communist, and "anarchist" trade unions. This fact alone shows that the tendency toward "growing together" is intrinsic not in this or that doctrine as such but derives from social conditions common for all unions.

Monopoly capitalism does not rest on competition and free private initiative but on centralized command. The capitalist cliques at the head of mighty trusts, syndicates, banking consortiums, and so on, view economic life from the very same heights as does state power; and they require at every step the collaboration of the latter. In their turn the trade unions in the most important branches of industry find themselves deprived of the possibility of profiting from the competition among the different enterprises. They have to confront a centralized capitalist adversary, intimately bound up with state power. Hence flows the need of the trade unions—insofar as they remain on reformist positions, that is, on positions of adapting themselves to private property—to adapt themselves to the capitalist state and to contend for its cooperation.

In the eyes of the bureaucracy of the trade union movement, the chief task lies in "freeing" the state from the embrace of capitalism, in weakening its dependence on trusts, in pulling it over to their side. This position is in complete harmony with the social position of the labor aristocracy and the labor bureaucracy, who fight for a crumb in the share of superprofits of imperialist capitalism. The labor bureaucrats do their level best in words and deeds to demonstrate to the "democratic" state how reliable and indispensable they are in peacetime and especially in time of war. By transforming the trade unions into organs of the state, fascism invents nothing new; it merely draws to their ultimate conclusion the tendencies inherent in imperialism.

Colonial and semicolonial countries are under the sway not of native capitalism but of foreign imperialism. However, this does not weaken but, on the contrary, strengthens the need of direct, daily, practical ties between the magnates of capitalism and the governments that are in essence subject to them: the governments of colonial or semicolonial countries. Inasmuch as imperialist capitalism creates both in colonies and semicolonies a stratum of labor aristocracy and bureaucracy, the latter requires the support of colonial and semicolonial governments as protectors, patrons, and sometimes as arbitrators. This constitutes the most important social basis for the Bonapartist and semi-Bonapartist character of governments in the colonies and in backward countries generally.[2] This likewise constitutes the basis for the dependence of reformist unions upon the state.

In Mexico the trade unions have been transformed by law into semistate institutions and have, in the nature of things, assumed a semitotalitarian character. The statization of the trade unions was, according to the conception of the legislators, introduced in the interests of the workers, in order to assure them an influence upon governmental and economic life. But insofar as foreign imperialist capitalism dominates the national state and insofar as it is able, with the assistance of internal reactionary forces, to overthrow the unstable democracy and replace it with outright fascist dictatorship, to that extent the legislation relating to the trade unions can easily become a weapon in the hands of imperialist dictatorship.

From the foregoing it seems, at first sight, easy to draw the conclusion that the trade unions cease to be trade unions in the imperialist epoch. They leave almost no room at all for workers' democracy which, in the good old days when free trade ruled on the economic arena, constituted the content of the inner life of labor organizations. In the absence of workers' democracy there cannot be any free struggle for influence over the trade union membership. And because of this, the chief arena of work for revolutionists within the trade unions disappears.

Such a position, however, would be false to the core. We cannot select the arena and the conditions for our activity to suit our own likes and dislikes. It is infinitely more difficult to fight in a totalitarian or a semitotalitarian state for influence over the working masses than in a democracy. The very same thing likewise applies to trade unions, whose fate reflects the change in the destiny of capitalist states. We cannot renounce the struggle for influence over workers in Germany merely because the totalitarian regime makes such work extremely difficult there. We cannot, in precisely the same way, renounce the struggle within the compulsory labor organizations created by fascism. All the less so can we renounce internal systematic work in trade unions of a totalitarian and semitotalitarian type merely because they depend directly or indirectly on the workers' state or because the bureaucracy deprives the revolutionists of the possibility of working freely within these trade unions.

It is necessary to conduct a struggle under all those concrete conditions that have been created by the preceding developments, including by the mistakes of the working class and the crimes of its leaders. In the fascist and semifascist countries it is impossible to carry on revolutionary work that is not underground, illegal, conspiratorial. Within the totalitarian and semitotalitarian unions it is impossible or well-nigh impossible to carry on any except conspiratorial work. It is necessary to adapt ourselves to the concrete conditions existing in the trade unions of every given country in order to mobilize the masses, not only against the bourgeoisie, but also against the totalitarian regime within the trade unions themselves and against the leaders enforcing this regime. The primary slogan for this struggle is: *complete and unconditional independence of the trade unions in relation to the capitalist state*. This means a struggle to turn the trade unions into the organs of the broad exploited masses and not the organs of a labor aristocracy.

❋

The second slogan is: *trade union democracy*. This second slogan flows directly from the first and presupposes for its realization the complete freedom of the trade unions from the imperialist or colonial state.

In other words, the trade unions in the present epoch cannot simply be the organs of democracy as they were in the epoch of free capitalism and they cannot any longer remain politically neutral, that is, limit themselves to serving the daily needs of the working class. They cannot any longer be anarchistic, that is, ignore the decisive influence of the state on the life of people and classes. They can no longer be reformist, because the objective conditions leave no room for any serious and lasting reforms. Either the trade unions of our time will serve as secondary instruments of imperialist capital to subordinate and discipline the workers and to obstruct the revolution or, on the contrary, the unions will become tools of the revolutionary movement of the proletariat.

✳

The neutrality of trade unions is completely and irretrievably a thing of the past—gone, together with free bourgeois democracy.

✳

From what has been said, it follows quite clearly that in spite of the progressive degeneration of trade unions and their growing together with the imperialist state, the work within the trade unions not only does not lose any of its importance but remains as before and becomes in a certain sense even more important work than ever for every revolutionary party. The matter at issue is essentially the struggle for influence over the working class. Every organization, every party, every faction that permits itself an ultimatistic position in relation to trade unions, that is, in essence turns its back upon the working class merely because of displeasure with its organization, every such organization is destined to perish. And it must be said that it deserves to perish.

✳

Inasmuch as the chief role in backward countries is played not by national but by foreign capitalism, the national bourgeoisie occupies, in the sense of its social position, a much more minor position than corresponds with the development of industry. Inasmuch as foreign capital does not import workers but proletarianizes the native population, the national proletariat soon begins playing the most important role in the life of the country. In these conditions the national government, to the extent that it tries to show resistance to foreign capital, is compelled to a greater or lesser degree to lean on the proletariat. On the other hand, the governments of those backward countries that consider it inescapable or more profitable for themselves to march shoulder to shoulder with foreign capital destroy the labor organizations and institute a more or less totalitarian regime.

Thus, the feebleness of the national bourgeoisie, the absence of traditions of municipal self-government, the pressure of foreign capitalism, and the relatively rapid growth of the proletariat cut the ground from under any kind of stable democratic regime. The governments of backward, that is, colonial and semicolonial countries by and large assume a Bonapartist or semi-Bonapartist character; they differ from one another in that some try to orient in a democratic direction, seeking support among workers and peasants, while others install a form close to military-police dictatorship.

This likewise determines the fate of the trade unions. They either stand under the special patronage of the state or they are subjected to cruel persecution. Patronage on the part of the state is dictated by two tasks that confront it: first to draw the working class closer, thus gaining a support for resistance against excessive pretensions on the part of imperialism; and, at the same time, to discipline the workers themselves by placing them under the control of a bureaucracy.

*

Monopoly capitalism is less and less willing to reconcile itself to the independence of trade unions. It demands of the reformist bureaucracy and the labor aristocracy, who pick up the crumbs from its banquet table, that they become transformed into its political police before the eyes of the working class. If that is not achieved, the labor bureaucracy is driven away and replaced by the fascists. Incidentally, all the efforts of the labor aristocracy in the service of imperialism cannot in the long run save them from destruction.

The intensification of class contradictions within each country, the intensification of antagonisms between one country and another, produce a situation in which imperialist capitalism can tolerate (that is, up to a certain time) a reformist bureaucracy only if the latter serves directly as a petty but active stockholder of its imperialist enterprises, of its plans and programs within the country as well as on the world arena. Social reformism must become transformed into social imperialism in order to prolong its existence—but only prolong it, and nothing more. Because along this road there is no way out in general.

Does this mean that in the epoch of imperialism independent trade unions are generally impossible? It would be fundamentally incorrect to pose the question this way. Impossible are the independent or semi-independent reformist trade unions. Wholly possible are revolutionary trade unions that not only are not stockholders of imperialist policy but that set as their task the direct overthrow of the rule of capitalism. In the epoch of imperialist decay the trade unions can be really independent only to the extent that they are conscious of being, in addition, the organs of proletarian revolution. In this sense the program of transitional demands adopted by the last congress of the Fourth International is not only the program for the activity of the party; in its fundamental features it is the program for activity of the trade unions.[3]

*

The development of backward countries is characterized by its combined character. In other words, the last word in imperialist technology, economics, and politics is combined in these countries with traditional backwardness and primitiveness. This law can be observed in the most diverse spheres of the development of colonial and semicolonial countries, including the sphere of the trade union movement. Imperialist capitalism operates here in its most cynical and naked form. It transports to virgin soil the most perfected methods of its tyrannical rule.

＊

In the trade union movement throughout the world there is to be observed in the last period a swing to the right and the suppression of internal democracy. In Britain the Minority Movement in the trade unions has been crushed (not without the assistance of Moscow); the leaders of the trade union movement are today, especially in the field of foreign policy, the obedient agents of the Conservative Party. In France there was no room for an independent existence for Stalinist trade unions. They united with the so-called anarcho-syndicalist trade unions under the leadership of Jouhaux, and as a result of this unification there was a general shift of the trade union movement not to the left but to the right. The leadership of the CGT is the most direct and open agency of French imperialist capitalism.[4]

In the United States the trade union movement has passed through the most stormy history in recent years. The rise of the CIO is incontrovertible evidence of the revolutionary tendencies within the working masses. Indicative and noteworthy in the highest degree, however, is the fact that the new "leftist" trade union organization was no sooner founded than it fell into the steel embrace of the imperialist state. The struggle among the tops between the old federation and the new is reducible in large measure to the struggle for the sympathy and support of Roosevelt and his cabinet.

No less graphic, although in a different sense, is the picture of the development, or the degeneration, of the trade union movement in Spain. In the Socialist trade unions all those leading elements that to any degree represented the independence of the trade union movement were pushed out. As regards the anarcho-syndicalist unions, they were transformed into the instrument of the bourgeois republicans; the anarcho-syndicalist leaders became conservative bourgeois ministers. The fact that this metamorphosis took place in conditions of civil war does not weaken its significance. War is the continuation of the selfsame policies. It speeds up processes, exposes their basic features, destroys all that is rotten, false, equivocal, and lays bare all that is essential. The shift of the trade unions to the right is due to the sharpening of class and international contradictions. The leaders of the trade union movement have sensed or understood, or have been given to understand, that now was no time to play the game of opposition. Every oppositional movement within the trade union movement, especially among the tops, threatens to provoke a stormy movement of the masses and to create difficulties for national imperialism. Hence flows the swing of the trade unions to the right and the suppression of workers' democracy within the unions. The basic feature, the swing toward the totalitarian regime, passes through the labor movement of the whole world.

We should also recall Holland. Not only did the reformist and the trade union movement there serve as a reliable prop of imperialist capitalism, but in addition the so-called anarcho-syndicalist organization there was actually under the control of the imperialist government. The secretary of this organization, Sneevliet, in spite of his platonic sympathies for the Fourth International, was, as a deputy in the Dutch parliament, most concerned lest the wrath of the government descend upon his trade union organization.

✳

In the United States the Department of Labor with its leftist bureaucracy has as its task the subordination of the trade union movement to the democratic state, and it must be said that this task has up to now been solved with some success.

✳

The nationalization of railways and oil fields in Mexico has, of course, nothing in common with socialism. It is a measure of state capitalism in a backward country, which in this way seeks to defend itself on the one hand against foreign imperialism and on the other against its own proletariat.[5] The management of railways, oil fields, etc., through labor organizations has nothing in common with workers' control over industry, for in the essence of the matter the management is effected through the labor bureaucracy, which is independent of the workers but, in return, completely dependent on the bourgeois state.

This measure on the part of the ruling class pursues the aim of disciplining the working class, making it more industrious in the service of the common interests of the state, which appear on the surface to merge with the interests of the working class itself. As a matter of fact, the whole task of the bourgeoisie consists in liquidating the trade unions as organs of the class struggle and substituting in their place the trade union bureaucracy as the organ of the leadership over the workers by the bourgeois state.

In these conditions the task of the revolutionary vanguard is to conduct a struggle for the complete independence of the trade unions and for the introduction of actual workers' control over the present union bureaucracy, which has been turned into the administration of railways, oil enterprises, and so on.

✳

Events of the last period (before the war) have revealed with especial clarity that anarchism—which in point of theory is always only liberalism drawn to its extremes—was, in practice, peaceful propaganda within the democratic republic whose protection it required. If we leave aside individual terrorist acts, etc., anarchism as a system of mass movement and politics presented only propaganda material under the peaceful protection of the law. In conditions of crisis the anarchists always did the opposite of what they taught in peacetime. This was pointed out by Marx himself in connection with the Paris Commune.

And it was repeated on a far more colossal scale in the experience of the Spanish revolution.

＊

Democratic unions in the old sense of the term—bodies where, in the framework of one and the same mass organization, different tendencies struggle more or less freely—can no longer exist. Just as it is impossible to bring back the bourgeois-democratic state, so is it impossible to bring back the old workers' democracy. The fate of the one reflects the fate of the other. As a matter of fact, the independence of the trade unions in the class sense, in their relations to the bourgeois state, can, in the present conditions, be assured only by a completely revolutionary leadership, that is, the leadership of the Fourth International. This leadership, naturally, must and can be rational and assure the unions the maximum of democracy conceivable under the present concrete conditions. But without the political leadership of the Fourth International the independence of the trade unions is impossible.

The question of trade union unity

In 1931, as a deep economic crisis broke over the capitalist world, communist opponents of Stalinism spoke as a public faction unjustly expelled from the Communist International. Organized in the International Left Opposition (Bolshevik-Leninists), they combated the Comintern's domination by the antirevolutionary, bureaucratic faction headed by Stalin and sought to put the International back on the communist course it had charted under Lenin's leadership.

France's labor movement had been split since 1921, when reformist leaders of the General Confederation of Labor (CGT), aligned with the Socialist Party, began expelling unions with a left-wing leadership. The expelled unions formed the Unitary General Confederation of Labor (CGTU). At its 1922 founding convention, the CGTU elected a revolutionary syndicalist leadership that included many members of the Communist Party.

In the late 1920s the Stalinist forces, who by this time headed the CGTU, adopted ultraleft and adventurist policies. They claimed that capitalism had entered its third, or final, period, to be followed shortly by world revolution. Communist parties around the world were instructed to split reformist-led trade unions and organize separate "Red" unions under Communist Party leadership.

The Monattists—the "unity brokers" in this article—were members of the Syndicalist League led by Pierre Monatte. Following World War I they had been part of the syndicalist grouping around the newspaper *La Vie Ouvrière* (which Monatte edited until 1922) and in the early 1920s joined the Communist Party. In the mid-1920s they broke first with Stalinism and then with communism altogether. Their evolution is the subject of part 2 of this book.

The question of the unity of the workers' organizations is not subject to a single solution suitable for all forms of organization and for all conditions.

For the party the question resolves itself in most categorical fashion. Its complete independence is the elementary condition of revolutionary action. But even this principle does not give in advance a ready-made reply to the question: When and under what conditions must a split or, contrariwise, a unification be made with a neighboring political current? Such questions are settled each time on the basis of a concrete analysis of the tendencies and political conditions. The highest criterion, in any case, remains the necessity for the vanguard of the organized proletariat, the party, to preserve its complete independence and autonomy on the basis of a distinct program of action.

But precisely such a solution of the question with regard to the party not only admits but, as a general rule, renders indispensable a quite different attitude with regard to the question of the unity of other mass organizations of the working class: trade unions, cooperatives, soviets.

Each one of these organizations has its own tasks and methods of work—and, within certain limits, independent ones. For the Communist Party, all these organizations are first of all the arena of revolutionary education of broad sections of the workers and recruitment of the advanced workers. The larger the mass in a given organization, the greater are the possibilities it offers the revolutionary vanguard. That is why, as a rule, it is not the Communist wing but the reformist wing that takes the initiative in splitting the mass organizations.

It is enough to contrast the conduct of the Bolsheviks in

1917 to that of the British trade unions in recent years. The Bolsheviks not only remained in the same trade unions with the Mensheviks, but in certain trade unions they tolerated a Menshevik leadership even after the October revolution, although the Bolsheviks had the overwhelming majority in the soviets. The British trade unions, on the contrary, upon the initiative of the Labourites, not only drive the Communists out of the Labour Party but, so far as it is possible, out of the trade unions as well.

In France the split in the trade unions was also the consequence of the initiative of the reformists, and it is no accident that the revolutionary trade union organization, compelled to lead an independent existence, adopted the name *unitary*.

Do we demand today that the Communists quit the ranks of the CGT? Not at all. On the contrary, the revolutionary wing within Jouhaux's confederation must be strengthened. But by that alone we show that the splitting of the trade union organization is in no case a question of principle for us. All the ultraleftist objections in principle that may be formulated against trade union unity apply first of all to the participation of Communists in the CGT. Yet every revolutionist who has not lost touch with reality must recognize that the creation of Communist fractions in the reformist trade unions is an extremely important task. One of the tasks of these fractions must be to defend the CGTU in discussions with members of the reformist trade unions. This cannot be accomplished except by showing that the Communists do not want the trade unions to be split but, on the contrary, are ready at any moment to reestablish trade union unity.

If one believes for an instant that the splitting of the trade unions is imposed on Communists by their duty to counterpose a revolutionary policy to the policy of the reformists, then one cannot limit oneself to France alone. One must demand that the Communists, regardless of the relationship of forces, break with the reformist trade unions and also set up their own trade unions in Germany, in Britain, in the United States, and so on.

In certain countries Communist parties have actually taken this road. In specific cases the reformists really leave no other way out. In other cases the Communists commit an obvious mistake by responding to the provocations of the reformists. But up to now Communists have never and nowhere motivated the splitting of the trade unions by the inadmissibility in principle of working with the reformists in the organizations of the proletarian masses.

Without stopping to deal with cooperatives—the experiences in which will add nothing essential to what has been said above—we will take soviets as an example.[6] These arise in the most revolutionary periods, when all problems are posed with the keenness of a blade. Can one, however, imagine even for a moment the creation of Communist soviets as a counterbalance to Social Democratic soviets? This would mean killing the very idea of the soviets.

At the beginning of 1917 the Bolsheviks remained within the soviets as an insignificant minority. For months—and in a period when months counted for years, if not for decades—the Bolsheviks tolerated a conciliationist [Menshevik and Socialist Revolutionary] majority in the soviets, even though they already represented an overwhelming majority in the factory committees. Finally, even after the conquest of power, the Bolsheviks tolerated the Mensheviks within the soviets so long as the Mensheviks represented a certain part of the working class. It was only when the Mensheviks had completely compromised and isolated themselves, by being transformed into a clique, that the soviets threw them out of their midst.

In Spain, where the slogan of soviets may in the near future be put practically on the order of the day, the very creation of soviets (juntas)—provided there is an energetic and bold initiative of the Communists—is not to be conceived of otherwise than by way of a technical organizational agreement with the trade unions and the Socialists on the method and the intervals of the election of workers' representatives. To advance, under these conditions, the idea of the inadmissibility of working with the reformists in the mass organizations would be one of the most disastrous forms of sectarianism.

＊

How then is such an attitude on our part toward the proletarian organizations led by the reformists to be reconciled with our evaluation of reformism as the left wing of the imperialist bourgeoisie? This contradiction is not a formal but a dialectical one, that is to say, one that flows from the very course of the class struggle. A considerable part of the working class (its majority in a number of countries) rejects our evaluation of reformism; in other countries, it has not as yet even approached this question. The whole problem consists precisely in leading these masses to revolutionary conclusions on the basis of our common experiences with them. We say to the noncommunist and to the anticommunist workers: "Today you still believe in the reformist leaders whom we consider to be traitors. We cannot and we do not wish to impose our point of view upon you by force. We want to convince you. Let us then endeavor to fight together and to examine the methods and the results of these fights." This means that within united trade unions, where union discipline applies to all members, groupings must enjoy full freedom.

No other principled position can be proposed.

＊

The Executive Committee of the Communist League [Left Opposition in France] is at present correctly giving first place to the question of the united front. This is the only way that one can prevent the reformists, and above all their left-wing agents, the Monattists, from counterposing to the practical tasks of the class struggle the formal slogan of unity.[7] [CP leader Albert] Vassart, as a counterbalance to the sterile official [Communist Party] line, has put forward the idea of the united front with the local trade union organizations. This way of posing the question is correct, in the sense that during local strikes it is primarily a question of working with local trade unions and specific [national] federations. It is equally true that the lower levels of the reformist apparatus are more sensitive to the pressure of the workers. But it would be wrong to make any kind of principled difference between agreements with the local opportunists and those with their chiefs. Everything depends upon the conditions of the moment, upon the strength of the pressure of the masses, and upon the character of the tasks that are on the order of the day.

It is self-evident that we never make agreement with the reformists, whether locally or centrally, an indispensable and preliminary condition for the struggle in each specific case. We orient ourselves not according to the reformists but according to the objective circumstances and the state of mind of the masses. The same applies to the character of demands put forward. It would be fatal for us to commit ourselves in advance to accept the united front according to the conditions of the reformists, that is, upon the basis of minimal demands. The working masses will not rise in struggle for demands that seem unrealistic to them. But on the other hand, should the demands be too limited in advance, the workers may say to themselves, "Why bother, it's not worth the trouble."

On each occasion, the task consists not in proposing the united front formally to the reformists but in forcing them to accept conditions that correspond as well as possible to the situation. All this calls for an active strategy, one of maneuver. In any case, it is incontestable that only in this way and by it alone can the CGTU mitigate, up to a certain point, the consequences of the division of the masses into two trade union organizations, throw the responsibility for the split onto those on whom it really belongs, and advance its own militant positions.

✳

The singularity of the situation in France lies in the fact that two trade union organizations have existed there separately for many years. In the face of the ebb of the movement in recent years, people have accustomed themselves to the split; very often it has simply been forgotten. However, one could foresee that the revival in the ranks of the working class would inevitably revive the slogan of the unity of the trade union organizations. If one takes into account that more than nine-tenths of the French proletariat is outside the trade unions, it becomes clear that, as the revival steps up, the pressure of the unorganized will increase. The slogan of unity is nothing but one of the first consequences of this pressure. With a correct policy, this pressure should be favorable to the Communist Party and the CGTU.

Even if, for the next period, an active united front policy were the principal method of the French Communists' trade union strategy, it would nonetheless be quite wrong to counterpose this policy to that of unity of the trade union organizations.

It is entirely incontestable that the unity of the working class can be realized only on a revolutionary basis. The policy of the united front is one of the means of liberating the workers from reformist influence and even, in the last analysis, of moving toward the genuine unity of the working class. We must constantly explain this Marxist truth to the advanced workers. But a historical perspective, even the most correct one, cannot replace the living experience of the masses. The party is the vanguard, but in its work, especially in its trade union work, it must be able to lean toward the rear guard. It must, in fact, show the workers—once, twice, and even ten times if necessary—that it is ready at any moment at all to help them reconstitute the unity of the trade union organizations. And in this field we remain faithful to the essential principles of Marxist strategy: combining the struggle for reforms with the struggle for revolution.

✳

What is the attitude today of the two trade union confederations toward unity? To the broad circles of the workers it must appear entirely identical. In truth, the administrative stratum of each organization has declared that unification can only be conceived of "from below" on the basis of that organization's principles. By covering itself with the slogan of unity from below, borrowed from the CGTU, the reformist confederation exploits the forgetfulness of the working class and the ignorance of the younger generation, which knows nothing of the splitting work of Jouhaux, Dumoulin, and company. At the same time the Monattists assist Jouhaux by substituting for the fighting tasks of the labor movement the single slogan of trade union unity. As honest brokers they direct all their efforts against the CGTU in order to detach from it the greatest possible number of trade unions, to group these around themselves, and then to enter into negotiations with the reformist confederation on an equal footing.

As far as I am able to judge here from the material I have, Vassart has expressed himself in favor of the Communists themselves putting forward the slogan of a unification congress of the two trade union confederations. This proposal was categorically rejected; as for its author, he was accused of having gone over to Monatte's position. Lacking data, I am unable to express myself thoroughly on this discussion. But I consider that the French Communists have no reason to abandon the slogan of a fusion congress. On the contrary.

The Monattists say, "They are both, one as much as the other, splitters. We alone are for unity. Workers, support us." The reformists reply, "As for us, we are for unity from below." That is, "we" will generously permit the workers to rejoin our organization. What must the revolutionary confederation say on this subject? "It is not for nothing that we call ourselves the unitary confederation. We are ready to effect the unity of the trade union organization this very day. But to accomplish that, the workers have no need whatsoever of questionable brokers who have no trade union organization behind them and who feed upon splits like maggots on a festering wound. We propose the preparation and, after a specified period, the convening of a fusion congress on the basis of trade union democracy."

This manner of posing the question would immediately cut the ground from under the feet of the Monattists, who are a completely sterile political grouping but are capable of bringing great confusion into the ranks of the proletariat. But will not elimination of the group of brokers in this way cost us too dearly? It will be objected that if the reformists consented to a unity congress, the Communists would be in the minority there and the CGTU would have to give way to the CGT.

Such a consideration can appear persuasive only to a left trade union bureaucrat who is fighting for his "independence" while losing sight of the perspectives and tasks of the movement as a whole. The unity of the two trade union organizations, even if the revolutionary wing remains in the minority for a time, would very quickly be revealed to be favorable precisely to communism and to it alone. The unity of the confederations would bring in its train a great influx of new members. Thanks to this, the influence of the [economic] crisis would be reflected within the trade unions in a more profound and more decisive fashion. The left wing would be able, within the rising new wave, to begin a decisive struggle for the conquest of the unified confederation. A preference for an assured majority in a narrow and isolated trade union confederation rather than oppositional work in a broad and real mass organization, is the mark only of sectarians or officials and not of proletarian revolutionists.

For a thinking Marxist it is quite evident that one of the factors contributing to the monstrous mistakes of the CGTU leadership resulted from a situation where people like Monmousseau, Sémard, and others, without theoretical preparation or revolutionary experience, immediately proclaimed themselves the "masters" of an independent organization [in 1922] and consequently had the possibility of experimenting with it under the orders of [Comintern leaders] Lozovsky, Manuilsky, and company. It is incontestable that if the reformists had not at some point brought about the split in the confederation, Monmousseau and company would have had to reckon with broader masses. This fact alone would have disciplined their bureaucratic adventurism. That is why the advantages of unity would have been immeasurably greater at present than the disadvantages. If, within a unified confederation embracing about a million workers, the revolutionary wing remained in the minority for a year or two, these two years would undoubtedly be more fruitful for the education not only of the Communist trade unionists but of the whole party than five years of "independent" zigzags in a CGTU growing constantly weaker.

*

No, it is not we but the reformists who should fear trade union unity. If they consented to a unity congress—not in words but in deeds—that would create the possibility of bringing the labor movement in France out of its blind alley. But that is just why the reformists will not consent to it.

The conditions of the crisis are creating the greatest difficulties for the reformists, primarily in the trade union field. That is why they find it so necessary to take shelter behind their left flank; it is the brokers of unity who offer them this shelter.

To unmask the splitting work of the reformists and the parasitism of the Monattists is now one of the most important and indispensable tasks. The slogan of the unity congress can contribute greatly to the solution of this task. When the Monattists speak of unity, they aim this slogan against the Communists; when the CGTU itself proposes a road to unity, it will deliver a mortal blow to the Monattists and will weaken the reformists. Isn't this quite clear?

It is true that we know in advance that, thanks to the resistance of the reformists, the slogan of unity will not yield the great results at present that would be obtained in the case of a real unity of the trade union organizations. But a more limited result, provided the Communists follow a correct policy, will undoubtedly be achieved. The broad masses of workers will see who is really for unity and who is against it, and will become convinced that the services of brokers are not required. There is no doubt that in the long run the Monattists will be reduced to nothing, the CGTU will feel itself stronger, and the CGT weaker and more unstable.

But if that is how matters stand, does this policy not boil down simply to a maneuver rather than to the achieving of effective unity? This objection cannot frighten us. This is precisely the way that the reformists evaluate our whole policy of the united front. They declare that our proposals are a maneuver only because they themselves do not want to lead the struggle.

It would be entirely false to differentiate in principle between the policy of the united front and that of the fusion of the trade union organizations. Provided that the Communists preserve the complete independence of their party, of their fraction in the trade unions, of their whole policy, the fusion of the confederations is nothing but a form of the policy of the united front, a more extended and broader form. In rejecting our proposal, the reformists transform it into a "maneuver." But on our part, it is a legitimate and indispensable "maneuver"; it is such maneuvers that train the working masses.

❋

The Executive Committee of the Communist League, we say again, is entirely correct when it urgently repeats that unity of action cannot be postponed until the unification of the trade union organizations. This idea must be developed as has been done heretofore, explained, and applied in practice. But this does not exclude the duty of posing boldly, at a definite and well-chosen moment, the question of the fusion of the [CGT and CGTU] confederations or even of individual [union] federations.

The whole question consists in knowing if the Communist leadership is now capable of effecting such a bold maneuver. The future will show. But if the [Communist] Party and the leadership of the CGTU refuse to follow the advice of the [Communist] League today—which is most probable—it may well be that they will be obliged to follow it tomorrow. It is super-fluous to add that we make no fetish of trade union unity. We postpone no question of struggle until unity. It is not a question for us of a panacea, but of a lesson in specific and important things that must be taught to the workers who have forgotten or who do not know the past.

*

For participation in the unity congress, we do not of course set any conditions of principle.

When the unity brokers, who are not ashamed of cheap phrases, say that the united confederation must base itself upon the principle of class struggle, etc., they are doing verbal acrobatics in the interests of the opportunists. As if a serious man could ask Jouhaux and company, in the name of unity with the Communists, to tread the road of the class struggle, which these gentlemen have deliberately abandoned in the name of unity with the bourgeoisie. And just what do these brokers themselves, all these Monattes, Zyromskys, and Dumoulins, understand by the "class struggle"? We are ready at any moment to stand on the grounds of trade union unity, but not in order to "correct" (with the aid of quack formulas) the mercenaries of capital. No, we take this stand in order to tear the workers away from their traitorous influence. The only conditions that we set have the character of organizational guarantees of trade union democracy, first of all the freedom of criticism for the minority, naturally on the condition that it submits to trade union discipline. We ask for nothing else, and on our part we promise nothing more.

*

Let us imagine that the [Communist] Party—even if not immediately—follows our advice. How should its Central Committee act? It would first of all be obliged to carefully prepare within the party the plan of campaign, to discuss it in all the trade union fractions in the light of local trade union conditions, so that the slogan of unity might be effectively directed simultaneously from above and from below. Only after careful preparation and elaboration, after having eliminated all doubts and misunderstandings within its own ranks, would the leadership of the CGTU address itself to the leadership of the reformist confederation with concretely elaborated proposals: to create a parity commission for the preparation, within a period of two months for example, of the trade union unification congress to which all the trade union organizations of the country must be admitted. Simultaneously, the local CGTU organizations address themselves to the local CGT organizations with the same proposal, formulated with precision and concreteness.

The Communist Party would develop a broad agitation in the country, supporting and explaining the initiative of the CGTU. The attention of the broadest circles of workers, and primarily that of the CGT workers, must for a certain time be concentrated on the simple idea that the Communists propose to achieve immediately the organizational unity of the trade union organizations. Whatever the attitude of the reformists may be, whatever may be the ruses to which they resort, the Communists will come out of this campaign with profit, even if their proposal comes to no more, in this first attempt, than a demonstration of their attitude.

The struggle in the name of the united front does not cease, during this period, for a single minute. The Communists continue to attack the reformists in the provinces and in the center, basing themselves upon the growing activity of the workers, renewing all their offers of fighting actions on the basis of the policy of the united front, unmasking the reformists, strengthening their own ranks, and so on. And it may well happen that in six months, in a year or two, the Communists will be obliged to repeat their proposal of fusion of the trade union confederations and thus put the reformists in a more difficult position than the first time.

A genuinely bolshevik policy must have precisely this character. It must boldly take the offensive while conducting a maneuver. It is only on this road that the movement can be preserved from stagnation and purged of parasitic formations, and the evolution of the working class toward revolution can be accelerated.

*

The lesson proposed above has no meaning and cannot succeed unless the initiative comes from the CGTU and the Communist Party. The task of the league naturally does not consist of independently advancing the slogan of a unity congress, pitting itself against the CGTU as well as against the CGT. The league's task is to push the official party and the CGTU onto the road of a bold united front policy and to stimulate them, on the basis of this policy, to carry out at a propitious moment—and in the future there will be many such moments—a decisive offensive for the fusion of the trade union organizations.

In order to fulfill its tasks toward the party, the league—and this is its first duty—must align its own ranks in the field of the trade union movement. It is a task that cannot be postponed. It must and will be solved.

September 4, 1933

The unions in Britain

Early in 1933, two years after Trotsky wrote "The Question of Trade Union Unity," fascism triumphed in Germany, crushing the workers' movement there. Trotsky explained that sectarian policies of the German Communist Party, which originated in the Communist International, were responsible for this disaster.

"The strategic conception of the Communist International was false from beginning to end," he wrote. "The point of departure of the German Communist Party was that there is nothing but a mere division of labor between the Social Democracy and fascism; that their interests are similar, if not identical. Instead of helping to aggravate the discord between Communism's principal political adversary and its mortal foe . . . the Communist International convinced the reformists and the fascists that they were twins. . . . In every case where, despite the obstacles presented by the leadership, local unity committees for workers' defense were created, the [Stalinist] bureaucracy forced its representatives to withdraw under threat of expulsion. . . . The capitulation of the reformists served the interests of fascism and not of Communism; the Social Democratic workers remained with their leaders; the Communist workers lost faith in themselves and in the leadership."[8]

During the months that followed, when the Communist International proved unable to correct this disastrous political course, Trotsky and the International Left Opposition concluded that the Comintern's degeneration could not be reversed. A new, revolutionary International was required.

"The Unions in Britain" is excerpted from "The ILP and the New International," available in *Writings of Leon Trotsky (1933–34)* (New York: Pathfinder, 1975), pp. 72–78.

The trade union question remains the most important question of proletarian policy in Great Britain, as well as in the majority of old capitalist countries. The mistakes of the Comintern in this field are innumerable. No wonder: a party's inability to establish correct relations with the working class reveals itself most glaringly in the area of the trade union movement. That is why I consider it necessary to dwell on this question.

The trade unions were formed during the period of the growth and rise of capitalism. They had as their task the raising of the material and cultural level of the proletariat and the extension of its political rights. This work, which in England lasted over a century, gave the trade unions tremendous authority among the workers.

The decay of British capitalism, under the conditions of decline of the world capitalist system, undermined the basis for the reformist work of the trade unions. Capitalism can continue to maintain itself only by lowering the standard of living of the working class. Under these conditions trade unions can either transform themselves into revolutionary organizations or become lieutenants of capital in the intensified exploitation of the workers. The trade union bureaucracy, which has satisfactorily solved its own social problem, took the second path. It turned all the accumulated authority of the trade unions against the socialist revolution and even against any attempts of the workers to resist the attacks of capital and reaction.

From that point on, the most important task of the revolutionary party became the liberation of the workers from the reactionary influence of the trade union bureaucracy. In this decisive field the Comintern revealed complete inadequacy. In 1926–27, especially in the period of the miners' strike and the general strike, that is, at the time of the greatest crimes and betrayals of the General Council of the Trades Union Congress, the Comintern obsequiously toadied to the highly placed strike-breakers, cloaked them with its authority in the eyes of the masses, and helped them remain in the saddle.[9] That is how the Minority Movement was struck a mortal blow.

Frightened by the results of its own work, the Comintern bureaucracy went to the extreme of ultraradicalism. The fatal excesses of the "third period" were due to the desire of the small Communist minority to act as though it had a majority behind it. Isolating itself more and more from the working class, the Communist Party counterposed to the trade unions, which embraced millions of workers, its own trade union organizations, which were highly obedient to the leadership of the Comintern but separated by an abyss from the working class. No better favor could be done for the trade union bureaucracy. Had it been within its power to award the Order of the Garter, it should have so decorated all the leaders of the Comintern and Profintern.

As was said, the trade unions now play not a progressive but a reactionary role. Nevertheless they still embrace millions of workers. One must not think that the workers are blind and do not see the change in the historic role of the trade unions. But what is to be done? The revolutionary road is seriously compromised in the eyes of the left wing of the workers by the zigzags and adventures of official communism. The workers say to themselves: The trade unions are bad, but without them it might be even worse. This is the psychology of one who is in a blind alley. Meanwhile, the trade union bureaucracy persecutes the revolutionary workers ever more boldly, ever more impudently replacing internal democracy by the arbitrary action of a clique, in essence transforming the trade unions into some sort of concentration camp for the workers during the decline of capitalism.

Under these conditions, the thought easily arises: Is it not possible to bypass the trade unions? Is it not possible to replace them by some sort of fresh, uncorrupted organization such as revolutionary trade unions, shop committees, soviets, and the like? The fundamental mistake of such attempts is that they reduce to organizational experiments the great political problem of how to free the masses from the influence of the trade union bureaucracy. It is not enough to offer the masses a new address. It is necessary to seek out the masses where they are and to lead them.

Impatient leftists sometimes say that it is absolutely impossible to win over the trade unions because the bureaucracy uses the organizations' internal regimes for preserving its own interests, resorting to the basest machinations, repressions, and plain crookedness, in the spirit of the parliamentary oligarchy of the era of "rotten boroughs."[10] Why then waste time and energy? This argument reduces itself in reality to giving up the actual struggle to win the masses, using the corrupt character of the trade union bureaucracy as a pretext.

This argument can be developed further: Why not abandon revolutionary work altogether, considering the repressions and provocations on the part of the government bureaucracy? There exists no principled difference here, since the trade union bureaucracy has definitely become a part of the capitalist apparatus, economic and governmental. It is absurd to think that it would be possible to work against the trade union bureaucracy with its own help, or only with its consent. Insofar as it defends itself by persecutions, violence, expulsions, frequently resorting to the assistance of government authorities, we must learn to work in the trade unions *discreetly,* finding a common language with the masses but not revealing ourselves prematurely to the bureaucracy. It is precisely in the present epoch, when the reformist bureaucracy of the proletariat has transformed itself into the economic police of capital, that revolutionary work in the trade unions, performed intelligently and systematically, may yield decisive results in a comparatively short time.

We do not at all mean by this that the revolutionary party has any guarantee that the trade unions will be completely won over to the socialist revolution. The problem is not so simple. The trade union apparatus has attained for itself great independence from the masses. The bureaucracy is capable of retaining its positions a long time after the masses have turned against it. But it is precisely such a situation, where the masses are already hostile to the trade union bureaucracy but where the bureaucracy is still capable of misrepresenting the opinion of the organization and of sabotaging new elections, that is most favorable for the creation of shop committees, workers' councils, and other organizations for the immediate needs of any given moment. Even in Russia, where the trade unions did not have anything like the powerful traditions of the British trade unions, the October revolution occurred with Mensheviks predominant in the administration of the trade unions. Having lost the masses, these administrations were still capable of sabotaging elections in the apparatus, although already powerless to sabotage the proletarian revolution.

It is absolutely necessary right now to prepare the minds of the advanced workers for the idea of creating shop committees and workers' councils at the moment of a sharp change. But it would be the greatest mistake to "play around" in practice with the slogan of shop councils, consoling oneself with this "idea" for the lack of real work and real influence in the trade unions. To counterpose to the existing trade unions the abstract idea of workers' councils would mean setting against oneself not only the bureaucracy but also the masses, thus depriving oneself of the possibility of preparing the ground for the creation of workers' councils.

In this the Comintern has gained not a little experience: having created obedient, that is, purely Communist trade unions, it counterposed its sections to the working masses in a hostile manner and thereby doomed itself to complete impotence. This is one of the most important causes of the collapse of the German Communist Party. It is true that the British Communist

Party, insofar as I am informed, opposes the slogan of workers' councils under the present conditions. Superficially, this may seem like a realistic appraisal of the situation. In reality, the British Communist Party rejects only one form of political adventurism for another, more hysterical form. The theory and practice of social fascism and the rejection of the policy of the united front create insurmountable obstacles to working in the trade unions, since each trade union is, by its very nature, the arena of an ongoing united front of revolutionary parties with reformist and nonparty masses.[11] To the extent that the British Communist Party proved incapable, even after the German tragedy, of learning anything and arming itself anew, to that extent can an alliance with it pull to the bottom even the Independent Labour Party (ILP), which only recently has entered a period of revolutionary apprenticeship.

Pseudocommunists will, no doubt, refer to the last congress of trade unions, which declared that there could be no united front with Communists against fascism. It would be the greatest folly to accept this piece of wisdom as the final verdict of history. The trade union bureaucrats can permit themselves such boastful formulas only because they are not immediately threatened by fascism or by communism. When the hammer of fascism is raised over the head of the trade unions, then, with a correct policy of the revolutionary party, the trade union masses will show an irresistible urge for an alliance with the revolutionary wing and will carry with them onto this path even a certain portion of the apparatus. Contrariwise, if communism should become a decisive force, threatening the General Council with the loss of positions, honors, and income, Messrs. Citrine and company would undoubtedly enter into a bloc with Mosley and company against the Communists.

Thus, in August 1917 the Russian Mensheviks and Socialist Revolutionaries together with the Bolsheviks repulsed General Kornilov. Two months later, in October, they were fighting hand in hand with the Kornilovists against the Bolsheviks. And in the first months of 1917, when the reformists were still strong, they spouted, just like Citrine and company, about the impossibility of their making an alliance with a dictatorship either of the right or left.

The revolutionary proletarian party must be welded together by a clear understanding of its historic tasks. This presupposes a scientifically based program. At the same time the revolutionary party must know how to establish correct relations with the class. This presupposes a policy of revolutionary realism, equally removed from opportunistic vagueness and sectarian aloofness. From the point of view of both these closely connected criteria, the ILP should review its relation to the Comintern as well as to all other organizations and tendencies within the working class. This concerns first of all the fate of the ILP itself.

Letters on the Dutch trade union situation

The following are excerpts from three letters by Trotsky. The first is addressed to the Central Committee of the Dutch Revolutionary Socialist Workers Party (RSAP); the second was sent to RSAP leader Henk Sneevliet, who also headed the National Labor Secretariat (NAS), a small left-wing trade union federation. The third letter is addressed to the International Secretariat, the leadership body of the Movement for a Fourth International. Complete texts are printed in "The Dutch Section and the International," in *Writings of Leon Trotsky (1935–36)* (New York: Pathfinder, 1977), pp. 362–76, and in "The Future of the Dutch Section" and "Conclusion of a Long Experience," in *Writings of Leon Trotsky (1937–38)* (New York: Pathfinder, 1976), pp. 81–83 and 150–52.

TO THE RSAP CENTRAL COMMITTEE
JULY 16, 1936

On the trade union question too I cannot share the policy of our fraternal Dutch party. The reasons for that I have often set forth in writing and especially verbally. The policy toward the NAS continues to be carried out only on the basis of the law of inertia. There is no deeper strategic motivation for it. Developments in Holland, just as is now the case in France, will have to strike out either on the revolutionary or the fascist road. In either case I see no place for the NAS. When the great strike wave begins in Holland, which should be regarded as highly probable if not certain, the reformist trade unions will grow mightily and absorb fresh elements into their ranks, and in such a period the NAS will appear to the masses as an incomprehensible splinter organization. In consequence, the masses will also become unresponsive to the correct slogans of the RSAP and the leadership of the NAS.

But if all the members of the RSAP and the best NAS elements were inside the reformist trade unions, then during the impending upsurge they could become the axis of crystallization of the left wing and, later on, the decisive force in the labor movement. I must say quite openly: systematic, solicitously arranged agitation inside the reformist trade unions seems to me the only means not only of preserving the RSAP as a genuinely independent party (for by itself this hasn't any historical value) but also of carrying it to victory, that is, to power.

If we take a much less probable alternative, namely, that developments in Holland, without passing through a revolutionary upsurge, go directly, in the coming period, into the reactionary military-bureaucratic and then into the fascist phase, we nevertheless come to the same conclusion: the NAS policy will inevitably become an obstacle to the party. The first assault of reaction has already been directed at the NAS and cost it half its membership.[12] The second assault will cost it its life. The excellent workers united within it will then have to seek the road into the reformist trade unions in a dispersed manner, everyone for himself, or else remain passive and indifferent. The trade union cannot lead the illegal existence that the party can. But by means of this blow the party will be terribly hit, for an illegal revolutionary party must have a legal or semilegal mass cover. If the bulk of the membership of the RSAP is active in the reformist trade unions, then these mass organizations mean for the party too a hiding place, a cover, and at the same time, an arena. The coherence of the present NAS workers is thereby preserved. All other points will be conditioned by the course of development and the policy of the party.

TO HENK SNEEVLIET

DECEMBER 2, 1937

You must finally understand that nobody in our international movement is inclined to further tolerate the absolutely abnormal situation under which the Dutch party covers itself with the banner of the Fourth International and conducts a policy that is flagrantly contradictory to all our principles and decisions.

The NAS has definitely become a stone around the neck of the party, and this stone will drag you to the bottom. A party that does not participate in the real trade unions is not a revolutionary party. The NAS exists thanks only to the toleration and financial support of the bourgeois government.[13] This financial support is dependent upon your political attitude. That is the genuine reason why the party did not, in spite of all our insistence, elaborate a political platform. That is also the reason why you, as parliamentary deputy, never gave a genuine revolutionary speech that could serve for propaganda in Holland as well as abroad. Your activity has a diplomatic and not a very revolutionary character. You are bound hand and foot by your NAS position. And the NAS itself is not a bridge to the masses but a wall separating you from the masses.

When we criticize false trade union politics in other countries, people answer, "And your Dutch organization?" ... Do you believe that any serious revolutionary organization can tolerate indefinitely such a situation? We are very patient, but we cannot sacrifice the elementary interests of our movement.

TO THE INTERNATIONAL SECRETARIAT
JANUARY 21, 1938

All that the International Secretariat has written about and against Sneevliet was and still is absolutely correct. That is precisely the reason why Sneevliet has never dared to respond with political arguments, utilizing instead—and this is his manner—abusive language that is absolutely intolerable and not at all justified. Sneevliet does not take the slightest interest in Marxism, in theories, in a general orientation. What interests him is the NAS, a tiny bureaucratic machine, a parliamentary post. Sneevliet utilizes the banner of the Fourth International above all in order to protect his opportunistic work in Holland. Since the NAS depends financially entirely upon the government, Sneevliet has evaded all precise politics, that is to say, Marxist politics, in order not to provoke the thunder of the government against the NAS. The RSAP has been and still is nothing more than a political appendage of the NAS, which itself is not viable and which has fallen in the last years from 25,000 to 12,000 members and very likely still lower.

Trade unions and factory committees

These sections on trade unions and factory committees are excerpted from "The Death Agony of Capitalism and the Tasks of the Fourth International." Often called the Transitional Program, this resolution was adopted in 1938 by the founding conference of the Fourth International. The complete text is available in *The Transitional Program for Socialist Revolution* (New York: Pathfinder, 1977).

Trade unions in the transitional epoch

In the struggle for partial and transitional demands, the workers now more than ever before need mass organizations, principally trade unions. The powerful growth of trade unionism in France and the United States is the best refutation of the preachments of those ultraleft doctrinaires who have been teaching that trade unions have "outlived their usefulness."

The Bolshevik-Leninist stands in the frontline trenches of all kinds of struggles, even when they involve only the most modest material interests or democratic rights of the working class. He takes active part in mass trade unions for the purpose of strengthening them and raising their spirit of militancy. He fights uncompromisingly against any attempt to subordinate the unions to the bourgeois state and bind the proletariat to "compulsory arbitration" and every other form of police guardianship—not only fascist but also "democratic." Only on the basis of such work within the trade unions is successful struggle possible against the reformists, including those of the Stalinist bureaucracy. Sectarian attempts to build or preserve small "revolutionary" unions, as a second edition of the party, signify in actuality the renouncing of the struggle for leadership of the working class. It is necessary to establish this firm rule: self-isolation of the capitulationist variety from mass trade unions, which is tantamount to a betrayal of the revolution, is incompatible with membership in the Fourth International.

At the same time, the Fourth International resolutely rejects and condemns trade union fetishism, equally characteristic of trade unionists and syndicalists.

(a) Trade unions do not offer and, in line with their task, composition, and manner of recruiting membership, cannot offer a finished revolutionary program; in consequence, they cannot replace the *party*. The building of national revolutionary parties as sections of the Fourth International is the central task of the transitional epoch.

(b) Trade unions, even the most powerful, embrace no more than 20 to 25 percent of the working class, and at that, predominantly the more skilled and better-paid layers. The more oppressed majority of the working class is drawn only episodically into the struggle, during a period of exceptional upsurges in the labor movement. During such moments it is necessary to create organizations ad hoc, embracing the whole fighting mass: strike committees, factory committees, and finally, soviets.

(c) As organizations expressive of the top layers of the proletariat, trade unions, as witnessed by all past historical experience, including the fresh experience of the anarcho-syndicalist unions in Spain, developed powerful tendencies toward compromise with the bourgeois-democratic regime. In periods of acute class struggle the leading bodies of the trade unions aim to become masters of the mass movement in order to render it harmless. This is already occurring during the period of simple strikes, especially in the case of the mass sit-down strikes, which shake the principle of bourgeois property. In time of war or revolution, when the bourgeoisie is plunged into exceptional difficulties, trade union leaders usually become bourgeois ministers.

Therefore, the sections of the Fourth International should always strive not only to renew the top leadership of the trade unions, boldly and resolutely in critical moments advancing new militant leaders in place of routine functionaries and careerists, but also to create in all possible instances independent militant organizations corresponding more closely to the tasks of mass struggle against bourgeois society; and if necessary, not flinching even in the face of a direct break with the conservative apparatus of the trade unions. If it be criminal to turn one's back on mass organizations for the sake of fostering sectarian fictions, it is no less so to passively tolerate subordination of the revolutionary mass movement to the control of openly reactionary or disguised conservative ("progressive") bureaucratic cliques. Trade unions are not ends in themselves; they are but means along the road to proletarian revolution.

Factory committees

During a transitional epoch, the workers' movement does not have a systematic and well-balanced, but a feverish and explosive character. Slogans as well as organizational forms should be subordinated to this feature of the movement. On guard against routine handling of a situation as against a plague, the leadership should respond sensitively to the initiative of the masses.

Sit-down strikes, the latest expression of this kind of initiative, go beyond the limits of "normal" capitalist procedure. In-

dependently of the demands of the strikers, the temporary seizure of factories deals a blow to the idol, capitalist property.
Every sit-down strike poses in a practical manner the question
of who is boss of the factory: the capitalist or the workers?

If the sit-down strike raises this question episodically, the
factory committee gives it organized expression. Elected by all
the factory employees, the factory committee immediately creates a counterweight to the will of the administration.

To the reformist criticism of bosses of the "economic royalist" type like Ford in contradistinction to "good," "democratic"
exploiters,[14] we counterpose the slogan of factory committees
as centers of struggle against both the first and the second.

Trade union bureaucrats will as a general rule resist the creation of factory committees, just as they resist every bold step
taken along the road of mobilizing the masses.

However, the wider the sweep of the movement, the easier
will it be to break this resistance. Where the closed shop has
already been instituted in "peaceful" times, the factory committee will formally coincide with the usual structure of the
trade union, but will renew its personnel and widen its func-
tions. The prime significance of the committee, however, lies in
the fact that it becomes the militant staff for such working-
class layers as the trade union is usually incapable of moving to
action. It is precisely from these more oppressed layers that the
most self-sacrificing battalions of the revolution will come.

From the moment that the committee makes its appearance,
a de facto dual power is established in the factory. By its very
essence it represents the transitional state, because it includes
in itself two irreconcilable regimes: the capitalist and the proletarian. The fundamental significance of factory committees is
contained precisely in the fact that they open the doors if not to
a direct revolutionary, then to a prerevolutionary period—between the bourgeois and the proletarian regimes. That the propa-
gation of the factory committee idea is neither premature nor
artificial is amply attested to by the waves of sit-down strikes
spreading through several countries. New waves of this type

will be inevitable in the immediate future. It is necessary to begin a timely campaign in favor of factory committees, in order not to be caught unawares.

Discussion with a CIO official

Trotsky based this article on two discussions at his home in Mexico with Abraham Plotkin (1892–1988), Midwest representative of the International Ladies' Garment Workers' Union, one of the U.S. unions belonging at the time to the Congress of Industrial Organizations.

CIO OFFICIAL: Our union's policies are aimed at preventing complete unemployment. We've got the work spread out among all the members of the union with no reduction in the hourly rate of pay.

TROTSKY: And what percentage of their former total wages do your workers now get?

CIO OFFICIAL: About 40 percent.

TROTSKY: Why that's monstrous! You've won a sliding scale of working hours with no change in the hourly rate of pay? But that only means that the full burden of unemployment falls with all its weight on the workers themselves. You free the bourgeoisie from the need of spending its resources on the unemployed by having each worker sacrifice three-fifths of his total wages.

CIO OFFICIAL: There's a grain of truth in that. But what can be done?

TROTSKY: Not a grain, but the whole truth! American capitalism is sick with a chronic and incurable disease. Can you console your workers with the hope that the present crisis will have a transitory character and that a new era of prosperity will open in the near future?

CIO OFFICIAL: Personally, I don't allow myself such illusions. Many in our circles understand that capitalism has entered its era of decline.

TROTSKY: But of course this means that tomorrow your workers will get 30 percent of their former wages; the day after, 25 percent; and so forth. Episodic improvements, it is true, are possible, even inevitable; but the overall curve is toward decline, degradation, impoverishment. Marx and Engels predicted this even in the Communist Manifesto. What is the program of your union and the CIO as a whole?

CIO OFFICIAL: Unfortunately, you don't know the psychology of the American workers. They are not used to thinking about the future. They are interested in only one thing: what can be done now, immediately. Among the leaders of the trade union movement there are, of course, those who clearly take into account the dangers that threaten. But they can't change the psychology of the masses all at once. The habits, traditions, and views of the American workers tie them down and limit what they can do. All this can't be changed in a day.

TROTSKY: Are you sure that history will provide you with years enough in which to prepare? The crisis of American capitalism has "American" tempos and proportions. A sturdy organism that has not known sickness before begins to deteriorate very rapidly at a certain point. The disintegration of capitalism means, at the same time, a direct and immediate threat to democracy, without which the trade unions cannot exist. Do you think, for example, that Mayor Hague[*] is just an accident?

CIO OFFICIAL: Oh no, I don't think so at all. I have had quite

---

[*] The mayor of Jersey City [New Jersey], who successfully applied purely fascistic methods against workers' organizations.—Leon Trotsky

a few meetings in the recent period with trade union officials on this subject. My opinion is that in every state we already have—under one banner or another—a ready-made reactionary organization that can become a support for fascism on the national level. We don't have to wait fifteen or twenty years. Fascism can conquer among us in three or four.

TROTSKY: In that case what is—?

CIO OFFICIAL: Our program? I understand your question. It is a difficult situation; some major steps are necessary. But I don't see the necessary forces or necessary leaders for this.

TROTSKY: Then does that mean capitulation without a fight?

CIO OFFICIAL: It's a difficult situation. I have to admit that the majority of union activists don't see, or don't want to see, the danger. Our unions, as you know, have had an extraordinary growth in a short time. It's natural for the CIO chiefs to have a honeymoon psychology. They are inclined to view difficulties lightly. The government not only has them figured out, but even plays with them. They are not used to this from past experience. It's natural that their heads spin a little. This pleasant dizziness is not conducive to critical thinking. They are tasting the joys of today without worrying about tomorrow.

TROTSKY: Well said! On this I agree with you completely. But the success of the CIO is temporary. It is merely a symptom of the fact that the working class of the United States has begun to move, has broken out of its routine, is hunting for new ways to save itself from the threatening abyss. If your unions do not find new ways, they will be ground to dust. Hague is already stronger than Lewis; because Hague, despite his limited situation, knows exactly what he wants, while Lewis doesn't. Things may end up with your chiefs waking from their "pleasant dizziness" to find themselves—in concentration camps.

CIO OFFICIAL: Unfortunately, the past history of the United States with its unlimited opportunities, its individualism, has not taught our workers to think socially. It's enough to tell you that at best 15 percent of the organized workers come to union meetings. That's something to think about.

TROTSKY: But perhaps the reason for the absenteeism of 85 percent is that the speakers have nothing to say to the ranks?

CIO OFFICIAL: Hmm. That's true to a certain extent. The economic situation is such that we are forced to hold back the workers, to put brakes on the movement, to retreat. This is not to the workers' liking, of course.

TROTSKY: Here we have the heart of the matter. It is not the ranks who are to blame but the leaders. In the classical epoch of capitalism the trade unions also got into difficult situations during crises and were forced to retreat, lost part of their membership, spent their reserve funds. But then there was at least the assurance that the next upturn would allow the losses to be made up, and more besides. Today there isn't the slightest hope for such a thing. The unions will go down step by step. Your organization, the CIO, may collapse as quickly as it arose.

CIO OFFICIAL: What can be done?

TROTSKY: Above all, one must tell the masses what's what. It's inadmissible to play hide-and-seek. You, of course, know the American workers better than I. Nevertheless, let me assure you that you are looking at them through old eyeglasses. The masses are immeasurably better, more daring and resolute than the leaders. The very fact of the rapid rise of the CIO shows that the American worker has changed radically under the impact of the terrible economic jolts of the postwar period, especially of the past decade. When you showed a little initiative in building more combative unions, the workers immediately responded and gave you extraordinary, unprecedented support. You have no right to complain about the masses.

And what about the so-called sit-down strikes? It wasn't the leaders who thought them up, but the workers themselves. Isn't this an unmistakable sign that the American workers are ready to go over to more decisive methods of combat? Mayor Hague is a direct product of the sit-down strikes. Unfortunately, no one in the top layer of the trade unions has yet dared to deduce from the sharpening of the social struggle such daring conclusions as capitalist reaction has. This is the key to the situation.

The leaders of capital think and act immeasurably more firmly, consistently, daringly, than do the leaders of the proletariat—these skeptics, routinists, bureaucrats, who are smothering the fighting spirit of the masses. It is from this that the danger grows of a victory for fascism, even in a very short time.

The workers don't come to your meetings because they instinctively feel the insufficiency, the lack of substance, the lifelessness, the outright falsity of your program. The trade union leaders give out platitudes at the very moment when every worker senses catastrophe overhead. One must find the language that corresponds to the real conditions of decaying capitalism and not to bureaucratic illusions.

CIO OFFICIAL: I have already said that I see no leaders. There are separate groups, sects, but I see no one who could unite the worker masses, even if I agree with you that the masses are ready for struggle.

TROTSKY: The problem is not leaders, but program. The correct program not only arouses and consolidates the masses, but also trains the leaders.

CIO OFFICIAL: What do you consider a correct program?

TROTSKY: You know that I am a Marxist; more precisely, a Bolshevik.

My program has a very short and simple name: *socialist revolution*. But I don't ask that the leaders of the union movement immediately adopt the program of the Fourth International. What I do ask is that they draw conclusions from their work, from their own situation; that for themselves and for the masses they answer just these two questions: (1) How to save the CIO from bankruptcy and destruction? (2) How to save the United States from fascism?

CIO OFFICIAL: What would you yourself do in the United States today if you were a trade union organizer?

TROTSKY: First of all, the trade unions should stand the question of unemployment and wages on its head. The sliding scale of hours, such as you have, is correct: everyone should have work. But the sliding scale of hours should be supplemented by a sliding scale of wages. The working class cannot permit a continuous lowering of its living standards, for this would be equivalent to the destruction of human culture. The highest weekly pay rates on the eve of the 1929 crisis must be taken as the point of departure. The mighty productive forces created by the workers have not disappeared nor been destroyed; they are there at hand. Those who own and control these productive forces are responsible for unemployment. The workers know how to work and want to work. The work should be divided up among all the workers. The weekly pay for each worker should be no less than the maximum attained in the past. Such is the natural, the necessary, the unpostponable demand of the trade unions. Otherwise they will be swept away like trash by historical developments.

CIO OFFICIAL: Is this program realizable? It means the certain ruin of the capitalists. This very program might hasten the growth of fascism.

TROTSKY: Of course this program means struggle and not prostration. The trade unions have two possibilities: either to maneuver, tack back and forth, retreat, close their eyes, and capitulate bit by bit in order not to "anger" the owners or "provoke" reaction. It was by this road that the German and Austrian Social Democrats and trade union officials tried to save themselves from fascism. The result is known to you: they cut their own throats. The other road is to understand the inexorable character of the present social crisis and to lead the masses to the offensive.

CIO OFFICIAL: But you still haven't answered the question about fascism, that is, the immediate danger that the trade unions draw down upon themselves by radical demands.

TROTSKY: I have not forgotten that for a moment. The fascist danger is already at hand, even before the appearance of radical demands. It flows from the decline and disintegration of capitalism. Granted that it might be strengthened for a while by the pressure of a radical trade union program. One must openly warn the workers of this.

One must set about creating special defense organizations in a practical way right now. There is no other road! You can no more save yourself from fascism with the help of democratic laws, resolutions, or proclamations than you can from a cavalry unit with the help of diplomatic notes. One must teach the workers to defend their lives and their future, arms in hand, from the gangsters and bandits of capital. Fascism grows swiftly in an atmosphere of immunity from punishment. One cannot doubt for a moment that the fascist heroes will turn with their tails between their legs when they realize that for each of their squadrons the workers are ready to send out two, three, or four squadrons of their own. The only way not just to save the workers' organizations but also to keep casualties to the minimum is to create a powerful organization of workers' self-defense in time. This is the trade unions' most important responsibility, if they do not wish to perish ingloriously. The working class needs a *workers' militia!*

CIO OFFICIAL: But what is the further perspective? Where will such methods of struggle get the trade unions in the last analysis?

TROTSKY: It is obvious that the sliding scale and workers' self-defense are not sufficient. These are just the first steps, necessary in order to protect the workers from death by starvation or the fascists' knives. These are urgent and necessary means of self-defense. But by themselves they will not resolve the problem. The basic task consists in laying the foundation for a better economic system, for a more just, rational, and decent utilization of the productive forces in the interests of all the people.

This can't be attained by the ordinary, "normal," routine methods of the trade unions. You cannot disagree with this, for in the conditions of capitalist decline isolated unions turn out to be incapable of halting even the further deterioration of the workers' conditions. More decisive and deep-going methods are necessary. The bourgeoisie, who hold sway over the means of production and who have state power, have brought the economy to a state of total and hopeless disarray. It is necessary to declare the bourgeoisie incompetent and to transfer the economy into fresh and honest hands, that is, into the hands of the workers themselves.

How to do this? The first step is clear: all the trade unions should unite and form their own *labor* party. Not the party of Roosevelt or La Guardia, not a "labor" party in name only,[15] but a truly independent political organization of the working class. Only such a party is capable of gathering around itself the ruined farmers, the small artisans, the shopkeepers. But for this it would have to wage an uncompromising struggle against the banks, trusts, monopolies, and their political agents, that is, the Republican and Democratic parties. The task of the labor party should consist in taking power into its own hands, all the power, and then putting the economy in order. This means organizing the entire national economy according to a single rational plan whose aim is not the profit of a small bunch of exploiters but the material and spiritual interests of a population of 130 million.

CIO OFFICIAL: Many of our activists are beginning to understand that the course of political development is moving toward a labor party. But Roosevelt's popularity is still too great. If he agrees to run for president a third time, the question of a labor party will have to be postponed another four years.

TROTSKY: There precisely is the tragedy resulting from the fact that Messrs. Leaders look to those above them instead of those below. The coming war, the decay of American capitalism, the growth of unemployment and poverty, all these basic processes, which directly determine the fate of dozens and hundreds of millions of people, do not depend on the candidacy or "popularity" of Roosevelt. I assure you that he is far more popular among the well-paid CIO officials than among the unemployed. Incidentally, the trade unions exist for the workers, not the officials.

If the idea of the CIO inspired millions of workers for a certain period, the idea of an independent, militant labor party that aims to put an end to economic anarchy, unemployment, and misery, to save the people and its culture, the idea of such a party is capable of inspiring tens of millions. Of course the agitators of the labor party would immediately have to show the masses, by word and deed, that they are not electoral agents of Roosevelt, La Guardia, and company, but true fighters for the interests of the exploited masses.

When the speakers talk in the language of workers' leaders and not of White House agents, then 85 percent of the members will come to meetings, while the 15 percent of conservative oldsters, worker-aristocrats, and careerists will stay away. The masses are better, more daring, more resolute than the leaders. The masses wish to struggle. Putting the brakes on the struggle are the leaders, who have lagged behind the masses. Their own indecisiveness, their own conservatism, their own bourgeois prejudices are disguised by the leaders with allusions to the backwardness of the masses. Such is the true state of affairs at present.

CIO OFFICIAL: Now, what you say has a lot of truth in it. But— well—we'll talk about that next time.

Part 2

Communism and syndicalism

Preface

BY FARRELL DOBBS

The subject of this section may be more or less new to readers just developing an interest in radical politics. Someone in that position, who sought a quick way of making a tentative comparison of the terms used in the title, might decide to look them up in a dictionary. In *Webster's New International Dictionary* he would find these definitions:

"*Communism* . . . a social and political doctrine or movement based upon revolutionary Marxian socialism that interprets history as a relentless class war eventually to result everywhere in the victory of the proletariat and the social ownership of the means of production with relative social and economic equality for all and ultimately to lead to a classless society."

"*Syndicalism* . . . a revolutionary political movement that aims by the general strike and direct action of labor unions to overthrow parliamentary democracy and establish a corporate society with general control in the hands of trade unions and workers' cooperatives."

Both of these dry, abstract definitions imply a working-class struggle for power in order to transform society. But they leave a big gap regarding vital questions of how that revolutionary aim is to be accomplished. It is precisely on those questions that Leon Trotsky takes the subject out of the realm of abstract generalities and, in a series of articles, counterposes communist and syndicalist views in terms of class-struggle realities. These articles, written in polemical form, center largely around the political evolution of the French syndicalist leader Monatte, a onetime revolutionary whose policies led him onto a false course.

Trotsky puts the question of communism and syndicalism into historical perspective. Latter-day syndicalism, he explains, represents the arrested development and retrogression of an earlier tendency that had moved part way onto the revolutionary road. The early syndicalists, who organized themselves in opposition to policies that brought the trade unions into collaboration with the capitalist ruling class, constituted an embryo of a revolutionary workers' party. Their political weakness lay in wrong views about the nature of the state and the role of the party in the struggle for workers' power. From these shortcomings arose their mistakes in tactics, such as one-sided preoccupation with the general strike as the central instrument for the transformation of society.

Revolutionary syndicalism found its further development and completion in the rise of the Communist movement (symbolized by the Bolshevik Party, as guided by Lenin and Trotsky, which led the Russian workers to revolutionary victory in 1917). With this advance the workers were enabled to unify program, organization, and tactics through their own revolutionary party and to go forward in a struggle for state power.

Around the central theme of the vital role of the revolutionary party, Trotsky polemicizes against syndicalist misconceptions about the question of state power. He takes up the subject of bureaucratism in its various forms of manifestation within the labor movement. Readers in this country should especially note his comments about the reactionary character of the native trade union bureaucracy and the lessons to be derived from the role of similar formations abroad. Taken in context with his remarks about the myth of politically "independent" trade unions, the analysis sheds light on fundamental aspects of contemporary working-class politics.

The original collection of articles on which this series is based, written by a master polemicist who had exceptional Marxist insight into the laws of class struggle, appeared across the years 1923 to 1931. The period was marked by the rise of Stalinism in the world Communist movement. That caused Trotsky, as leader of the Left Opposition, to include in the series some pertinent material on communist policy in the trade unions. Although the material relates specifically to earlier historical conditions, the basic concepts set forth retain full validity and constitute a valuable guide for worker-militants today.

An introduction to the first edition of this pamphlet was written in 1931 by James P. Cannon, founding leader of the Trotskyist movement in the United States.[16] One of his concerns at the time was the skepticism in this country about the Communist movement among militants with a syndicalist background. He said to them, "But, granting serious defects in the party, what is to be done about it? As we see the thing—since we proceed from the point of view that a party cannot be dispensed with—one must either struggle to reform the party or, if he thinks it is hopeless, form a new one. We, the Opposition, have taken the former course."

The policy he described of working to reform the Communist parties of the Third International was later changed by the Left Opposition. The turn came when Stalinism's false policy helped deliver the German workers into Hitler's hands in 1933. With that catastrophe it became clear that Stalinism had so bankrupted the Third International that its former revolutionary vitality could not be restored. The situation required the building of new national parties in opposition to the Stalinized Communist parties and the uniting of the reconstructed parties into a new revolutionary International.

This new course led in 1938 to the launching of the Fourth International and, in this country, to the formation of the Socialist Workers Party. Although prevented by antidemocratic legislation from belonging to the Fourth International, the Socialist Workers Party shares its general political outlook.

Later on Cannon wrote a pamphlet about the syndicalists of the Industrial Workers of the World in which he drew the lessons of their experiences. In a separate but broadly interrelated work he made a study of the early socialist movement centered around Eugene V. Debs. These two pamphlets contribute greatly to an understanding of the perspectives and problems involved in building a revolutionary working-class party.[17]

Syndicalism is not a significant tendency within this country's trade unions today, but there are notions of a comparable nature within the "New Left." These notions stem from blind and sweeping rejection of the "Old Left" and, along with it, all the hard-won historical lessons about the decisive role of a Bolshevik-type party. This leads to improvisations of policy and action that can only wind up repeating the syndicalist mistakes of the past.

Attempts to turn the clock back by reviving syndicalist-type views can have only reactionary significance for the labor and radical movement. Trotsky shows why in practice that would mean the dissolution of the revolutionary vanguard into the politically backward mass of the broad, amorphous trade unions. Such a course contradicts the workers' need for conscious guidance on firmly established principles. It cuts across the task of forging the necessary leadership by uniting vanguard elements in the party of the proletarian revolution. As history has proven, a disciplined combat party is the only instrument that can stand against the organized opposition of the capitalist ruling class and its repressive apparatus, the state.

✳

The two articles dated 1923 were written shortly after Pierre Monatte and his revolutionary syndicalist group had joined the Communist Party of France. The next two, written in 1929, take up the discussion again six years later, when Monatte was retreating to his old position and away from communism. "Monatte Crosses the Rubicon," in 1930, draws a balance sheet of the discussion with the syndicalists after their bloc with a reformist wing of the union movement. The last article, in 1931, deals with problems of Marxist policy in the unions then being discussed by the French section of the International Left Opposition.

1969

July 31, 1920

Letter to a French syndicalist on the Communist Party

This letter was intended for Pierre Monatte, editor of the syndicalist newspaper *La Vie Ouvrière,* and was printed in its columns. Monatte, together with Alfred Rosmer, had led a revolutionary current in the labor movement that struggled for an internationalist course during World War I. In 1920 these forces were strongly attracted to the example of the Bolshevik-led revolution in Russia and to the Comintern, the Third International. Rosmer had gone to Moscow, where he helped prepare the Comintern's Second Congress.

Trotsky's letter was written during the Second Congress, at which a crucial discussion was under way between the international Communist leadership and prominent syndicalists from more than half a dozen countries. By the end of the debate, most of the syndicalist delegates had come to support the Comintern.[18]

Monatte and some other leading French revolutionaries could not attend the congress. They were in a French prison awaiting trial for "anarchist intrigues" and for threatening state security because of their involvement in a massive strike movement there in May 1920.

Dear friend,

You are in great doubt regarding the Third International, in view of its political and party character. You are afraid that the French syndicalist movement may be taken in tow by a political party. Allow me to express my views on the subject.

First of all I must say that the French syndicalist movement, whose independence is causing you such anxiety, is already completely in the tow of a political party. Naturally, neither Jouhaux nor his nearest assistants Dumoulin, Merrheim, and others are members of parliament as yet, and formally are not members of any political party. But this is simply a division of labor. In fact Jouhaux is carrying on the same *policy* of coalition with the bourgeoisie, in the domain of the syndicalist movement, as the French Socialism of the Renaudel-Longuet type is carrying on in parliament. Should the executive committee of the present Socialist Party be requested to lay out a program for the General Confederation of Labor and appoint its leading personnel, there is no doubt that the party would approve the present program of Jouhaux-Dumoulin-Merrheim and allow these gentlemen to continue to occupy their posts. Should Jouhaux and company be elected as members of parliament, and Renaudel and Longuet placed at the head of the [General] Confederation of Labor, nothing whatever would be changed in the internal life of France or in the fate of the French working class. You certainly will not deny this.

The above-mentioned circumstances prove, however, that it is not a question of parliamentarism or antiparliamentarism, or of formal party membership. All the old labels are worn out and do not correspond to the new contents. Jouhaux's antiparliamentarism resembles Renaudel's parliamentary cretinism as much as one drop of water resembles another. Official syndicalism may repudiate the party—for the sake of tradition—as much as it likes, but the bourgeois parties of France, in the secret depths of their hearts, can wish for no better representative at the head of the French syndicalist movement than Jouhaux, as they cannot wish for any better "Socialist" parliamentarians than Renaudel-Longuet. Naturally the bourgeoisie criticizes and blames them, but only in order not to weaken their position in the labor movement.

The proletariat's revolutionary goal

The heart of the matter lies not in parliamentarism or in syndicalism—these are only forms—but in the substance of the policy that the vanguard of the working class is carrying out through the unions, as well as in parliament. A bonafide communist policy—a policy directed toward the overthrow of the rule of the bourgeoisie and its state—will find its revolutionary expression in all branches of life of the working class, in all organizations, institutions, and organs that its representatives are able to penetrate: in unions, mass meetings, in the press, in Communist Party organizations, in secret revolutionary circles working in the army or preparing an uprising, and, lastly, from the parliamentary rostrum, if the advanced workers elect a bonafide revolutionary representative.

The task of the working class is to expel the bourgeoisie from power, annihilate its apparatus of violence and oppression, and create organs of its own labor dictatorship in order to crush resistance on the part of the bourgeoisie and reconstruct all social relations in the spirit of communism as soon as possible. Whoever, under the pretext of anarchism, does not acknowledge this task—*the dictatorship of the proletariat*—is not a revolutionary but a petty-bourgeois grumbler. There is no place for him in our midst. We will come back to this later.

Hence the task of the proletariat consists in suppressing the bourgeois order by means of a revolutionary dictatorship. But in the working class itself, as you know, there are different levels of class consciousness. The task of the communist revolution is clear in its totality only to the most advanced revolutionary minority of the proletariat. The strength of this minority lies in the fact that the more firmly, the more decisively and assuredly it acts, the more support it finds on the part of the numerous and more backward masses of workers. It is necessary, however, that the working class should be led *in all as-*

pects of life by its best, most class-conscious representatives, who always remain true to their colors and are always ready to give up their lives for the cause of the working class. In this way millions of workers mired in the prejudices of capitalism, the church, democracy, and so forth, will not lose their way but will find true expression of their desire for complete emancipation.

Need for a Communist party

You, the revolutionary French syndicalists, have approached the question correctly in stating that unions encompassing the broad masses of workers are not by themselves sufficient for the revolution, and that an *active minority* is necessary to educate the masses and give them a definite program of action in each concrete case.

What must such an active minority be? It is clear that it cannot be based on regional or trade union distinctions. The question is not one of advanced metalworkers, railwaymen, or joiners, but of the most advanced proletarians of the whole country. They must unite, draw up a definite program of action, strengthen their unity with firm internal discipline, and thus secure their leading influence over the whole struggle of the working class, all its organizations, and first and foremost, over the trade unions.

What, then, would you call this active minority of the proletariat, united by the communist program and prepared to lead the working class to storm the fortress of capital? We call it the Communist Party.

"But," you might say, "in such a case this party has nothing in common with the present French Socialist Party." You are absolutely right. That is why, to make the difference stand out, we speak of a Communist party, not of a Socialist party.

"However, you are still speaking of a *party*."

Yes, I am speaking of a *party*. Certainly, one might most successfully prove that the word *party* has been greatly compromised by parliamentarians, professional chatterboxes, petty-bourgeois charlatans, and on and on. But this relates not only to the word *party*. We are already agreed that the labor unions (French *syndicats*, English *trade unions*, German *Gewerkschaften*) have been sufficiently compromised by the shameful role that they, in the person of their leaders, played during the war, and for the most part are playing now. That is not, however, a reason for repudiating the word *union*. You will agree that the question lies not in terminology but in the substance of the matter. Under the heading *Communist Party* we understand the proletarian vanguard united in the name of dictatorship of the proletariat and communist revolution.

Arguments directed against politics and the party very often conceal an anarchistic noncomprehension of the state's role in the class struggle. Proudhon used to say the workshop *(l'atelier)* would make the state disappear. This is correct only in the sense that future society will become a gigantic workshop, liberated from all state elements, because the state is a coercive organization of class rule whereas under the communist order there will be no classes. The question now, however, is: *By what path* will we arrive at a communist social order? Proudhon thought that by uniting together, the workshops would gradually supplant capitalism and the state. This proved purely utopian: the workshop was supplanted by powerful factories, and over the latter rose the monopolizing trust.

The French syndicalists thought, and even now partly think, that the unions as such would suppress all capitalist property and abolish the bourgeois state. But this is not correct. Unions are a powerful weapon in a general strike because the means and methods of a general strike coincide with those of union organizations. But for a strike to actually become a general strike, an active minority is necessary to carry on revolutionary educational work day by day, hour by hour among the masses. Clearly this minority must be grouped not around craft or union characteristics but around a definite program of proletarian revolutionary action. This, as we have said, is the Communist Party.

It must be said, however, that history has known general strikes almost without unions, for example, the Russian October strike in 1905. On the other hand, the attempts of the French unions [in July 1919 and May 1920] to organize a general strike have failed up to now precisely because of the absence in France of a leading revolutionary organization, a Communist party, which day by day would have systematically prepared the uprising of the proletariat, and not simply attempted from time to time to improvise decorative mass demonstrations.

Inadequacy of trade union methods of struggle

But a general strike, which may be conducted best through the union apparatus, is not sufficient to overthrow bourgeois rule. A general strike is a means of defense, not a means of offense. We, on the other hand, have to bring down the bourgeoisie, wrench the state apparatus out of its hands. The bourgeoisie, through its state, is supported by the army. Only an open uprising, in which the proletariat collides face to face with the army, carrying the best part with it and dealing cruel blows to the counterrevolutionary elements—only such an open uprising of the proletariat can make it master of the situation in a country.

An uprising, however, requires energetic, intense preparatory work of an agitational, organizational, technical nature. Day in and day out the crimes and infamies of the bourgeoisie in all areas of public life must be denounced. International policies that perpetrate savage atrocities in the colonies, the internal despotism of the capitalist oligarchy, the baseness of the bourgeois press—all this must serve as material for a genuine revolutionary denunciation, with all the revolutionary conclusions that flow from it. These themes extend beyond the organizational framework and tasks of a union organization.

In addition, it is necessary to create organized support for the uprising of the proletariat. In each union local, at each factory, in every workshop there must be a group of workers bound closely together by common ideas and capable at the decisive moment, by stepping forward united, of carrying the masses with them, showing them the right path, guarding against mistakes, and guaranteeing victory.

It is necessary to penetrate the army. There must be a closely welded group of revolutionary soldiers in every regiment, ready and capable of going over to the side of the people at the moment of collision, rallying the whole regiment to follow them. These groups of revolutionary proletarians, organized and united by common ideas, can act with complete success only as nuclei of a single, centralized Communist party.

If we were able to have genuine friends, open and secret, in various governmental as well as military institutions—friends who would be informed of all events, all the plans and machinations of the ruling cliques, and would keep us informed—this would naturally be of great advantage to us. In the same way we would only strengthen our own position if we could send just a handful of workers into parliament, workers loyal and true to the cause of the communist revolution, working in close unity with the legal and illegal organizations of our party, absolutely subordinate to party discipline, playing the part of scouts of the revolutionary proletariat in parliament—one of the political general headquarters of the bourgeoisie—and ready at any moment to exchange the parliamentary rostrum for the barricades.

Certainly, dear friend, this is not a role for Renaudel, nor Sembat, nor Varenne. But we have Karl Liebknecht, do we not? He also was a member of parliament. The capitalists and social-patriotic rabble tried to drown his voice. But the few words of denunciation and appeal that he succeeded in throwing out over the heads of the German oppressors awakened the class consciousness and conscience of hundreds of thousands of German workers. Karl Liebknecht went from parliament to Potsdam Square, calling the proletarian masses to an open struggle. From Potsdam Square he was taken to prison; from there he went on to the barricades of the revolution. An ardent partisan of soviet power and the dictatorship of the proletariat, he considered it necessary to take part in the elections to the German Constituent [National] Assembly, and at the same time he was organizing communist soldiers. He perished at his revolutionary post.[19]

Who was Karl Liebknecht? A syndicalist? Parliamentarian? Journalist? No, he was a revolutionary Communist, someone who finds his way to the proletariat through all obstacles. Karl Liebknecht appealed to the unions, denouncing the German Jouhauxs and Merrheims. He conducted the work of the party among soldiers, preparing the insurrection. He published revolutionary newspapers and appeals, legal and illegal. He went into parliament to serve the same cause that at other hours he served in secret.

Organs of the proletarian dictatorship

As long as the best elements of the French proletariat have not created for themselves a centralized Communist party, they cannot take state power, they cannot suppress the bourgeois police, the bourgeois army, and private ownership of the means of production. Without all this, however, the workshop can never supplant the state. Whoever has not mastered this, after the Russian revolution, is altogether hopeless.

But even after the proletariat has conquered state power through a victorious insurrection, it will not be possible to liquidate the state immediately by transferring executive power to the unions. Unions are the organizers of the higher strata of workers by trade and by industry. The ruling power must voice the revolutionary interests and needs of the working class as a whole. That is why the organ of proletarian dictatorship must be soviets, not unions. Soviets will be elected by all the workers, including millions who never belonged to any union and have been awakened for the very first time by the revolution.

It is not enough, however, to merely create soviets. The soviets must carry out a definite revolutionary policy. They must be able to distinguish clearly between friends and foes. They must be capable of decisive, and, if need be, relentless measures. As the experience of the Russian as well as the Hungarian and

Bavarian revolutions shows, the bourgeoisie does not lay down its arms after the first defeat.[20] On the contrary, when it begins to see how much it has lost, despair doubles and triples its energy. The soviet regime is a regime of harsh struggle against counterrevolution, domestic and foreign. Who will be able to give the soviets, elected by workers at different levels of class consciousness, a clear and determined action program? Who will help them find their way in the confused and tangled international situation and choose the right road? Clearly, only the most class-conscious, most experienced, advanced proletarians, bound together by a homogeneous program. That is the Communist Party.

Some simpletons (or perhaps they are the sly ones) point out with horror that in Russia the party is "in command" of the soviets and unions. "The French unions," say some syndicalists, "demand independence, and they will not allow any party to be in command." How then, dear friend, I repeat, do the French unions allow Jouhaux to be in command—a direct agent of French and American capital? The formal independence of the French unions does not save them from being under the command of the bourgeoisie. The Russian unions abandoned such independence. They overthrew the bourgeoisie, driving the Russian Jouhauxs, Merrheims, and Dumoulins from their midst and replacing them with loyal, experienced, and reliable fighters: Communists. Thus they guaranteed not only their independence but their victory over the bourgeoisie.

It is true that our party leads the unions and the soviets. Was it always so? No, our party won its leading position through unrelenting struggle against the petty-bourgeois parties, the Mensheviks, Socialist Revolutionaries, as well as nonparty, that is, backward or unprincipled, elements. The Mensheviks, whom we have overthrown, say we assure our majorities by "force." But how is it that the working masses—who overthrew the rule of the tsar and then of the bourgeoisie and the coalition government, although they all held the state apparatus of force—how is it that they now not only suffer the "enforced" power of the Communist Party, leading the soviets, but are even entering our ranks in ever greater numbers? This is to be explained solely by the fact that during the course of the last years the Russian working class has passed through a great experience, has had occasion to verify in practice the policy of the various parties, groups, cliques, and to compare their words and actions, and thus come to the final conclusion that the only party that has remained true to itself at all moments of the revolution, in adversity and success, was and remains the Communist Party. It is only natural that at every election meeting of working men and women, at every union conference, the masses elect Communists to the most responsible posts. This determines the leading role of the Communist Party.

Revolutionary unity

At the present moment, the revolutionary syndicalists—or, more precisely, communists—like Monatte, Rosmer, and others, constitute a *minority* within the trade unions. They are in the opposition, criticizing and denouncing the machinations of the ruling majority, which is carrying through reformist, that is to say, purely bourgeois, tendencies. The French communists occupy the same position within the Socialist Party, which supports the ideas of petty-bourgeois reformism.

Do Monatte and Jouhaux pursue the same syndicalist policy? No, they are enemies. One serves the proletariat, the other supports bourgeois tendencies in a masked form. Do Loriot and Renaudel-Longuet pursue the same policy? No, one is leading the proletariat to a revolutionary dictatorship, the other is subordinating the working masses to a national bourgeois democracy.

In what, then, does the policy of Monatte differ from that of Loriot? In one thing only: Monatte is operating in the trade union field, Loriot chiefly in political organizations. But it is only a simple division of labor. Bonafide revolutionary syndicalists, like bonafide revolutionary socialists, must unite in a Communist party. They must cease being an opposition within other organizations that are fundamentally alien to them. As an independent organization adhering to the banner of the Third International, they must stand face to face with the broader masses, giving clear and precise answers to all their questions, leading their entire struggle and steering it onto the road of communist revolution.

Trade union, cooperative, and political organizations, the press, illegal circles in the army, the parliamentary rostrum, municipal councillors, and so on—these are merely different forms of organization, practical methods, different points of support. The struggle remains the same as to its substance, whatever branch it may occupy. The bearer of this struggle is the working class. Its leading vanguard, however, is the Communist Party, in which the truly revolutionary syndicalists should occupy a place of honor.

Yours,

L. Trotsky

A necessary discussion with our syndicalist comrades

In December 1920 the French Socialist Party congress at Tours voted to join the Communist International, adopting the name Communist Party. A minority, labeled Dissidents, walked out, soon establishing a new Socialist Party. Many of the leaders of the Communist Party had not fully accepted the political and organizational ideas of the Communist International, and during 1921 and 1922 an internal struggle flared up in the party. The Fourth Congress of the Comintern, held late 1922, adopted three resolutions on the situation in the French party.[21] Many right-wing members of the Communist Party leadership, including General Secretary Louis-Oscar Frossard, left the party in disagreement with these decisions.

Simultaneously, greater agreement was achieved with the revolutionary syndicalists grouped around *La Vie Ouvrière*. One continuing difference was the Communists' proposal that the CGTU affiliate to the Red International of Labor Unions (RILU), the international federation of revolutionary trade unions founded in July 1921 under the Comintern's leadership. The revolutionary syndicalists objected in particular to the fact that the RILU chose representatives to be part of the Comintern's Executive Committee, and in turn accepted Comintern representatives into its leading body. The syndicalists argued that this procedure subordinated the unions to a political party. One proponent of this view was Robert Louzon, a contributor to *La Vie Ouvrière* who was also a leader of the Communist Party.

At its November-December 1922 congress, the RILU dropped the provisions linking it organically to the Comintern, a concession aimed at removing an unnecessary obstacle to unity with the CGTU and other syndicalist bodies. The CGTU then joined the trade union International.

This article was written immediately after the Fourth World Congress of the Communist International as a reply to the arguments of Comrade Louzon. But at that time more attention was being devoted to the struggle against the Socialist right, against the last batch of Dissidents—Verfeuil, Frossard, and others. In this struggle our efforts were, and continue to be, united with those of the syndicalists, and I preferred to postpone the publication of this article.

We are firmly convinced that our excellent understanding with the revolutionary syndicalists will not cease to exist. The entrance of our old friend Monatte into the Communist Party was a great day for us. The revolution needs men of this kind. But it would be wrong to pay for a rapprochement with a confusion of ideas. In the course of recent months, the Communist Party of France has been purified and consolidated; hence we can enter into a tranquil and friendly discussion with our syndicalist comrades, side by side with whom we shall have much work to do and many battles to fight.

Comrade Louzon, in a series of articles and personal explanations, presented views with regard to the fundamental question of the relations between party and trade union that differ radically from the opinions of the Communist International and from Marxism. French comrades whose opinion I am accustomed to respect speak with great esteem of Comrade Louzon and his devotion to the proletariat. It is all the more necessary, therefore, to correct the errors made by him in such an important question. Comrade Louzon defends the complete and unqualified independence of the trade unions. Against what? Obviously against certain attacks. Whose? Against attacks ascribed to the party. Trade union autonomy, an indisputable necessity, is endowed with a certain absolute and almost mystical significance by Louzon. And our comrade here appeals, quite wrongly, to Marx.

The trade unions, says Louzon, represent the "working class as a whole." The party, however, is only a party. The working class as a whole cannot be subordinated to the party. There is not even room for equality between them. "The working class has its aim within itself." The party, however, can either serve the working class or be subordinated to it. Thus the party cannot "annex" the working class. The mutual representation of the Communist International and the Red International of Labor Unions [on each other's leading bodies], which existed until the last Moscow congresses, signifies, according to Louzon, the actual equalization of party and class. This mutual representation has now been abolished. The party thereby resumes its role of servant again. Comrade Louzon approves of this. According to him, this was also the standpoint of Marx. The end of the mutual representation of the political and trade union Internationals is, to Louzon, the rejection of the errors of Lassalle (!) and of the Social Democrats (!) and a return to the principles of Marxism.

This is the essence of an article that appeared in *La Vie Ouvrière* of December 15. The most astonishing thing in this and other similar articles is that the writer is obviously, consciously, and determinedly shutting his eyes to what is actually going on in France. One might think that the article had been written from the star Sirius. How else is it possible to understand the assertion that the trade unions represent the "working class as a whole"? Of what country is Louzon talking? If he means France, the trade unions there, so far as we are informed, do not, unfortunately, include even half of the working class. The criminal maneuvers of the reformist trade unionists, supported on the left by a few anarchists, have split the French trade union organization. Neither of the two trade union confederations embraces more than 300,000 workers. Neither singly nor together are they entitled to identify themselves with the whole of the French proletariat, of which they form only a modest part. Moreover, each trade union organization pursues a different policy. The reformist trade union federation works in cooperation with the bourgeoisie; the Unitary General Confederation of Labor is, fortunately, revolutionary. In the latter organization, Louzon represents but one tendency.

What then does he mean by the assertion that the working class, which he obviously regards as synonymous with the trade union organization, bears its own aim in itself? With whose help, and how, does the French working class express this aim? With the help of Jouhaux's organization? Certainly not. With the help of the CGTU? The CGTU has already rendered great services. But unfortunately it is not yet the whole working class. Finally, to mention everything, it was not so long ago that the CGTU was led by the anarcho-syndicalists of the "Pact." At the present time its leaders are syndicalist communists.[22] In which of these two periods has the CGTU best represented the interests of the working class? Who is to judge?

If we now attempt, with the aid of the international experience of *our party,* to answer this question, then, in Louzon's opinion, we commit a mortal sin, for we then demand that the party judge what policy is most beneficial to the working class. That is, we place the party above the working class. But if we were to turn to the *working class as a whole,* we would unfortunately find it divided, impotent, and mute. The different parts of the class, organized into different confederations, even different trade unions in the same confederation, and even different groups in the same trade union, would all give us different replies. But the overwhelming majority of the proletariat standing outside both trade union confederations would, at the present time, give us no reply at all.

There is no country in which the trade union organization embraces the whole working class. But in some countries it comprises at least a very large section of the workers. This, however, is not the case in France.

If, as Louzon opines, the party must not "annex" the working class (what is this term actually supposed to mean?), then for what reason does Comrade Louzon accord this right to syndicalism? He may reply, "Our trade union organization is still weak. But we do not doubt its future and its final victory." To this we should reply, "Certainly; we too share this conviction. But we have just as little doubt that the party, too, will win the unqualified confidence of the great majority of the working class."

Neither for the party nor for the trade unions is it a question of "annexing" the proletariat. (It is wrong for Louzon to employ the terminology customarily used by our opponents in their fight against the revolution.) It is a question of *winning the confidence* of the proletariat. And it is possible to do this only with correct tactics, tested by experience. Where and by whom are these tactics consciously, carefully, and critically prepared? Who suggests them to the working class? Certainly they do not fall from heaven. And the working class as a whole, as a "thing in itself," does not teach us these tactics either. It seems to us that Comrade Louzon has not faced this question.

"The working class has its aim within itself." If we strip this sentence of its mystical trappings, its obvious meaning is that the historic tasks of the proletariat are determined by its social position as a class and by its role in production, in society, and in the state. This is beyond dispute. But this truth does not help us answer the question with which we are concerned, namely: How is the proletariat to arrive at *subjective insight* into the historic task posed by its objective position? Were the proletariat as a whole capable of grasping its historic task immediately, it would need neither party nor trade union. Revolution would be born simultaneously with the proletariat. But in actuality the *process* by which the proletariat gains an insight into its historic mission is very long and painful, and full of internal contradictions.

It is only in the course of long struggles, severe trials, many vacillations, and extensive experience that insight as to the right ways and methods dawns upon the minds of the best elements of the working class, the vanguard of the masses. This applies equally to party and trade union. The trade union also begins as a small group of active workers and grows gradually as its experience enables it to gain the confidence of the masses. But while the revolutionary organizations are struggling to gain influence in the working class, the bourgeois ideologists counterpose the "working class as a whole" not only to the party of the working class but to its trade unions, which these ideologists accuse of wanting to "annex" the working class. *Le Temps* writes this whenever there is a strike. In other words, the bourgeois ideologists counterpose the working class as object to the working class as conscious subject. For it is only through its class-conscious minority that the working class gradually becomes a factor in history.

We thus see that the criticism leveled by Comrade Louzon against the "unwarranted claims" of the party *applies equally well to the "unwarranted claims" of the trade unions.* Above all in France, because French syndicalism—we must repeat this—was and is, in its organization and theory, likewise a *party.* This is also why it arrived, during its classical period (1905–7), at the theory of the "active minority," and not at the theory of the "collective proletariat." For what else is an active minority, held together by the unity of their ideas, if not a party? And on the other hand, would not a trade union mass organization not containing a class-conscious active minority be a purely formal and meaningless organization?

The fact that French syndicalism was a *party* was fully confirmed by the split that took place as soon as divergences in political viewpoints appeared in its ranks. But the party of revolutionary syndicalism fears the aversion felt by the French working class for parties as such. Therefore it has not assumed the *name* of party and has remained incomplete as regards organization. It is a party that attempted to have its members blend into the trade union membership, or at least take cover behind the trade unions. The actual subordination of the trade unions to certain tendencies, factions, and even cliques of syndicalism is thus explained. This is also the explanation of the Pact, which is a Masonic caricature of a party within the bosom of the trade union organization. And vice versa: the Communist International has most determinedly combated the split in the trade union movement in France, that is, its actual conversion into syndicalist parties. The main consideration of the Communist International has been the historic task of the working class as a whole, and the enormous independent significance of the trade union organization for solving the tasks of the proletariat. In this respect the Communist International has from its very inception defended the real and living independence of the trade unions in the spirit of Marxism.

Revolutionary syndicalism, which was in France in many respects the precursor of present-day communism, has acknowledged the theory of the active minority, that is, of the party, but without openly becoming a party. It has thereby prevented the trade unions from becoming if not an organization of the whole working class (which is not possible in a capitalist system), at least one of its broad masses.

The Communists are not afraid of the word *party*, for their party has nothing in common, and will have nothing in common, with the other parties. Their party is not one of the political parties of the bourgeois system; it is the active, class-conscious minority of the proletariat, its revolutionary vanguard. Hence the Communists have no reason, either in their ideology or their organization, to hide themselves behind the trade unions. They do not misuse the trade unions for machinations behind the scenes. They do not split the trade unions when they are a minority in them. They do not in any way disturb the independent development of the trade unions. And they support trade union struggles with all their strength.

But at the same time the Communist Party reserves the right to express its opinion on all questions in the working-class movement including the trade union question, to criticize trade union tactics, and to make definite proposals to the trade unions, which, on their part, are at liberty to accept or reject these proposals. The party strives to win the confidence of the working class, above all, of that section organized in the trade unions.

What is the meaning of the quotations from Marx adduced by Comrade Louzon?[23] It is a fact that Marx wrote in 1868 that the workers' party would emerge from the trade unions. When writing this he was thinking mainly of Britain, at that time the sole developed capitalist country already possessing extensive labor organizations. Half a century has passed since then. Historical experience has in general confirmed Marx's prophecies so far as Britain is concerned. The British Labour Party has actually been built up on the foundation of the trade unions. But does Comrade Louzon really think that the British Labour Party, as it is today, led by Henderson and Clynes, can be looked upon as representative of the interests of the proletariat as a whole? Most decidedly not. The Labour Party in Great Britain betrays the cause of the proletariat just as the trade union bureaucracy betrays it, although in Britain the trade unions come closer to comprising the working class as a whole than anywhere else.

On the other hand, we cannot doubt but that our Communist influence will grow in this British Labour Party that emerged from the trade unions, and that this will help render more acute the struggle between the masses and leaders within the trade unions until the treacherous bureaucrats are ultimately driven out and the Labour Party is completely transformed and regenerated. And we, like Comrade Louzon, belong to an International that includes the small British Communist Party but combats the Second International, which is supported by the British Labour Party that had its origin in the trade unions.

In Russia—and in the law of capitalist development Russia is exactly the antipode of Great Britain—the Communist Party, the former Social Democratic Party, is older than the trade unions and created the trade unions. Today the trade unions and the workers' state in Russia are completely under the influence of the Communist Party, which by no means had its origin in the trade unions but which, on the contrary, created and trained them. Will Comrade Louzon contend that Russia has evolved in contradiction to Marxism?

Is it not simpler to say that Marx's judgment on the origin of the party in the trade unions has been proved by experience to have been correct for Britain—and even there not 100 percent correct—but that Marx never had the slightest intention of laying down what he himself once scornfully designated as a "suprahistorical" law? All the other countries of Europe, including France, stand between Great Britain and Russia on this question. In some countries the trade unions are older than the party, in others the contrary has been the case; but nowhere, except in Britain and partially in Belgium, has the party of the proletariat emerged from the trade unions. In any case, no Communist party has developed organically out of the trade unions. But are we to deduce from this that the entire Communist International is of illegitimate birth?

When the British trade unions alternately supported the Conservatives and the Liberals and represented to a certain extent a labor appendage to these parties, when the political organization of the German workers was nothing more than a left wing of the democratic party, when the followers of Lassalle and Eisenach were quarreling among themselves,[24] Marx demanded the independence of the trade unions from all parties. This formula was dictated by the desire to counterpose the labor organizations to all bourgeois parties, and to prevent their being too closely bound up with socialist sects.

But Comrade Louzon may perhaps remember that it was Marx who founded the First International as well, the object of which was to guide the labor movement in all countries, in every respect, and to render it fruitful. This was in 1864 and *the International created by Marx was a party*. Marx refused to wait until the international party of the working class formed itself in some way out of the trade unions. He did his utmost to strengthen, within the trade unions, the influence of the ideas of scientific socialism—ideas first expressed in 1847 in the Communist Manifesto.

When Marx demanded for the trade unions complete independence from all existing parties and sects, that is, from all the bourgeois and petty-bourgeois parties and sects, he did this in order to make it easier for scientific socialism to gain dominance in the trade unions. Marx never saw in the party of scientific socialism one of the existing political parties—parliamentary, democratic, etc. For Marx the International was the class-conscious working class, represented at that time by a still very small vanguard.

If Comrade Louzon were consistent in his trade union metaphysic and in his interpretation of Marx, he would say, "Let us renounce the Communist Party and wait till this party arises out of the trade unions." That kind of logic would be fatal, not only for the party but for the union. Actually, the present French trade unions can regain their unity and win decisive influence over the masses only if their best elements are constituted in the class-conscious revolutionary vanguard of the proletariat, that is, in a Communist party.

Marx gave no final answer to the question of the relations between party and trade unions, and indeed he could not do so. For these relations are dependent on the varying circumstances in each separate case. Whether the party and the trade union confederation are mutually represented on their central committees, or whether they form joint committees of action as needed, is a question of no decisive importance. The forms of organization may alter, but the fundamental role of the party remains constant. The party, if it be worthy of the name, includes the whole vanguard of the working class and uses its ideological influence for rendering every branch of the labor movement fruitful, especially the trade union movement. But if the trade unions are worthy of their name, they include an ever-growing mass of workers, many backward elements among them. But they can fulfill their task only when consciously guided on firmly established principles. And they can have this leadership only when their best elements are united in the party of proletarian revolution.

The recent purification of the Communist Party of France, which rid itself on the one hand of whining petty bourgeois, of drawing-room heroes, of political Hamlets and sickening careerists, and on the other hand brought about the rapprochement of Communists and revolutionary syndicalists, implies a great stride toward the creation of suitable relations between trade union organizations and the political organization, which in turn means a great advance for the revolution.

Anarcho-syndicalist prejudices again!

This article was an answer to "Trade Unions and Party" by Robert Louzon. Both articles were published in *International Press Correspondence*, June 14, 1923.

Comrade Louzon's new article contains more errors than his earlier ones, although this time his main line of argument takes an entirely different turn.

In his former articles Comrade Louzon's starting points were abstractions that assumed that the trade unions represented the "working class as a whole." In my reply I put forward the question: Where does Comrade Louzon write his articles, in France or on Sirius? In his latest article Comrade Louzon deserts the shaky foundation of universal laws and attempts to stand upon the national ground of French syndicalism. Yes, he says, the French trade unions are not actually the working class as a whole, but only the active minority of the working class. That is, Comrade Louzon acknowledges that the trade unions form a sort of revolutionary party. But this syndicalist party is distinguished by being purely proletarian in its constituents; here lies its tremendous advantage over the Communist Party. And it has still another advantage: the syndicalist party categorically rejects the bourgeois state institutions; it does not "recognize" democracy and thus takes no part in parliamentary struggles.

Comrade Louzon is never weary of repeating that we are dealing with the peculiarities of French development and with these alone. Beginning with a broad generalization, in the course of which he transformed Marx into a syndicalist, Louzon now sets Britain, Russia, and Germany apart. He does not reply to our question on why he himself belongs to the Communist International in company with the small British Communist Party, and not to the Second International in company with the British trade unions and the British Labour Party supported by them. Louzon begins with a suprahistorical law for all countries and closes by claiming an exceptional law for France.

In this new form Louzon's theory bears a purely national character. More than this, its essential character excludes the possibility of an International. How can common tactics be spoken of unless there are common fundamental premises? It is certainly very difficult to understand why Comrade Louzon belongs to the Communist International. It is no less difficult to understand why he belongs to the French Communist Party, since there exists another party possessing all the advantages of the Communist Party and none of its drawbacks.

But though Comrade Louzon leaves international ground for the sake of national, he systematically ignores that "national" question put to him in our former article: What about the role played by the CGT during the war? The role played by Jouhaux was by no means less treacherous and despicable than that played by Renaudel. The sole difference consisted in the fact that the social-patriotic party arranged its views and actions in accordance with a certain system, while the trade union patriots acted purely empirically and veiled their actions in wretched and stupid improvisations. It may be said that as regards patriotic betrayal, the Socialist Party with its definite character surpassed the semidefinite syndicalist party. At bottom Jouhaux was at one with Renaudel.

And how is it today? Does Louzon desire the union of the two confederations? We desire it. The International deems it necessary. We should not be alarmed even if the union were to give Jouhaux the majority. Naturally we would not say—as does Comrade Louzon—that syndicalism, although headed by Jouhaux, Dumoulin, Merrheim, and the like, is the purest form of proletarian organization, that it embodies "the working class as a whole," and so on and so forth, for such a phrase would be a travesty of the facts. But we should consider the formation of a larger trade union organization—that is, the concentration of greater proletarian masses, forming a wider battlefield for the struggle for the ideas and tactics of communism—to be a greater gain for the cause of revolution. But for this the first necessity is that the ideas and tactics of communism do not remain in midair but are organized in the form of a party.

With regard to Comrade Louzon, he does not pursue his thoughts to the end, but his logical conclusion would be to substitute for the party a trade union organization of the "active minority." The inevitable result of this would be a substitute party and substitute trade union, for those trade unions required by Comrade Louzon are too indefinite for the role of a party and too small for the role of a trade union.

Comrade Louzon's arguments—to the effect that the trade unions do not want to soil their fingers by contact with the organs of bourgeois democracy—already form a weak echo of anarchism. It may be assumed that the majority of the workers organized in the CGTU will vote in the elections for the Communist Party (at least we hope that Comrade Louzon, as a member of the Communist Party, will call upon them to do so), while the majority of the members of the Yellow confederation will vote for the Blum-Renaudel party.[25] The trade union as a form of organization is not adapted for parliamentary struggle, but the workers organized in the trade unions will nevertheless have their deputies. It is simply a case of division of labor on the same class foundation.

Or, perchance, is what happens in parliament a matter of indifference to the French worker? The workers do not think so. The trade unions have frequently reacted to the legislative work of parliament and will continue to do so in the future. And if there are, at the same time, Communist deputies in parliament itself who work hand in hand with the revolutionary trade unions against the deeds of violence and blows of imperialist "democracy," this is naturally a plus and not a minus. French tradition says that deputies are traitors. But the Communist Party has been called into being for the express purpose of doing away with all tradition. Should any deputy think of retreating from the class line, he will be thrown out of the party. Our French party has learned how to do this, and all distrust in it is completely unfounded.

Louzon complains that the party contains many petty-bourgeois intellectuals. This is so. But the Fourth Congress of the Communist International recognized and adopted resolutions on this, and the resolutions have not been without effect. Further work is required to establish the proletarian character of the party. We shall, however, attain this end not with the self-contradictory trade union metaphysics of Comrade Louzon, but with systematic party work in the sphere of the trade unions and every other sphere of proletarian struggle. There is already a considerable number of workers on the Central Committee of our French party. This is mirrored in the whole party. The same tendency is at work, in accordance with the resolutions passed by the Fourth Congress, in parliamentary and municipal elections. By this the party will win the confidence of the revolutionary proletariat. And this means that the party will less and less lack really competent and active proletarians to occupy the most important and responsible revolutionary posts. I greatly fear that Comrade Louzon's views may exercise a retarding influence on this profound progressive evolution of the vanguard of the French working class. But I have no doubt that communism will succeed in overcoming this obstacle like all others.

October 14, 1929

Communism and syndicalism

Introduction to a discussion

In 1924 Pierre Monatte and Alfred Rosmer were expelled from the French Communist Party because of their support for Trotsky and the opposition he led in the Soviet party. They established a newspaper, *La Révolution Prolétarienne,* which united left-wing critics of the bureaucratic regime in the French party. Some of these oppositionists, like Rosmer, held to their communist views, while others, like Monatte, reverted to purely syndicalist positions. In 1926 many of these latter forces formed the Syndicalist League, whose stated aim was to reunite the CGT and CGTU on the basis of class-struggle principles and independence from political parties.

In 1928 and 1929, the heavy-handed intervention of the Communist Party leadership in CGTU affairs, together with a marked decline in CGTU membership, produced substantial opposition currents. At the September 1929 congress, a minority influenced by the Syndicalist League obtained 209 votes to 1,364 for the CGTU leadership. At about this time, forces close to the Syndicalist League formed the Committee for Trade Union Independence within the CGTU, based on unions of dockworkers, food workers, and printers.

The trade union question is one of the most important for the labor movement and, consequently, for the [Left] Opposition.

Without a precise position on the trade union question, the Opposition will be unable to win real influence upon the working class. That is why I believe it necessary to submit here, *for discussion*, a few considerations on the trade union question.

The party and the unions

1. The Communist Party is the fundamental weapon of revolutionary action of the proletariat, the combat organization of its vanguard. It must rise to the role of leader of the working class in all the spheres of its struggle without exception, and consequently in the trade union field.

2. Those who, in principle, counterpose trade union autonomy to the leadership of the Communist Party, counterpose thereby—whether they want to or not—the most backward proletarian section to the vanguard of the working class, the struggle for immediate demands to the struggle for the complete liberation of the workers, reformism to communism, opportunism to revolutionary Marxism.

Revolutionary syndicalism and communism

3. Prewar French syndicalism in the epoch of its rise and expansion, by fighting for trade union autonomy, actually fought for its independence from the bourgeois government and its parties, among them that of reformist-parliamentary socialism. This was a struggle against opportunism and for a revolutionary road.

Revolutionary syndicalism did not, in this connection, make a fetish of the autonomy of the mass organizations. On the contrary, it understood and preached the leading role of the revolutionary minority in relation to the mass organizations, which reflect the working class with all its contradictions, its backwardness, and its weaknesses.

4. The theory of the active minority was, in essence, an uncompleted theory of a proletarian party. In all its practice, revolutionary syndicalism was an embryo of a revolutionary party as against opportunism, that is, it was a remarkable draft out-

line of revolutionary communism.

5. The weakness of anarcho-syndicalism, even in its classical period, was the absence of a correct theoretical foundation and, as a result, a wrong understanding of the nature of the state and its role in the class struggle—an incomplete, not fully developed, and consequently wrong conception of the role of the revolutionary minority, that is, the party. Thence the mistakes in tactics such as fetishism of the general strike, ignoring the connection between the uprising and the seizure of power, and so forth.

6. After the war, French syndicalism found not only its refutation but also its development and its completion in communism. Attempts to revive revolutionary syndicalism now would be to try to turn back history. For the labor movement such attempts can have only reactionary significance.

The epigones of syndicalism

7. The epigones of syndicalism transform (in words) the independence of the trade union organization from the bourgeoisie and the reformist socialists into *independence in general*, into *absolute* independence from all parties, the Communist Party included.

If, in the period of expansion, syndicalism considered itself a vanguard and fought for the leading role of the vanguard minority among the backward masses, the epigones of syndicalism now fight against the identical wishes of the Communist vanguard, attempting, even though without success, to base themselves upon the lack of development and the prejudices of the more backward sections of the working class.

8. Independence from the influence of the bourgeoisie cannot be a passive state. It can express itself only by political acts, that is, by the struggle against the bourgeoisie. This struggle must be inspired by a distinct program, which requires organization and tactics for its application. It is the union of program, organization, and tactics that constitutes the party. In this way the real independence of the proletariat from the bourgeois

government cannot be realized unless the proletariat conducts its struggle under the leadership of a revolutionary and not an opportunist party.

9. The epigones of syndicalism would have one believe that the trade unions are sufficient by themselves. Theoretically this means nothing, but in practice it means the dissolution of the revolutionary vanguard into the backward masses, that is, the trade unions.

The larger the mass embraced by the trade unions, the better they are able to fulfill their mission. A proletarian party, on the contrary, merits its name only if it is ideologically homogeneous, bound by unity of action and organization. To represent the trade unions as self-sufficient because the proletariat has already attained its "majority" is to flatter the proletariat, to picture it other than it is and can be under capitalism. Capitalism keeps enormous masses of workers in ignorance and backwardness, leaving only the vanguard of the proletariat the possibility of breaking through all the difficulties and arriving at a clear comprehension of the tasks of its class as a whole.

The party's leading role does not infringe on genuine union autonomy

10. The real, practical, and not metaphysical autonomy of trade union organization is not in the least disturbed nor is it diminished by the struggle of the Communist Party for influence. Every member of the trade union has the right to vote as he thinks necessary and to elect the one who seems to him most worthy. Communists possess this right in the same way as others.

The conquest of the majority by the Communists in the leading bodies takes place quite in accordance with the principles of autonomy, that is, the self-administration of the trade unions. On the other hand, no trade union statute can prevent or prohibit the party from electing the general secretary of the labor confederation to its Central Committee, for here we are entirely in the domain of the autonomy of the party.

11. In the trade unions the Communists, of course, submit to the discipline of the party no matter what posts they occupy. This does not exclude but presupposes their submission to trade union discipline. In other words, the party does not impose upon them any line of conduct that contradicts the state of mind or the opinions of the majority of the members of trade unions. In entirely exceptional cases, when the party considers impossible the submission of its members to some *reactionary* decision of the trade union, it points out openly to its members the consequences that flow from it, that is, removals from trade union posts, expulsions, and so forth.

With juridical formulas in these questions—and autonomy is a purely juridical formula—one can get nowhere. The question must be posed in its essence, that is, on the plane of trade union *policy*. A correct policy must be counterposed to a wrong policy.

The character of the party's leading role depends on the conditions

12. The character of the party's leading role, its methods and forms, can differ profoundly in accordance with the general conditions of a given country or with the period of its development.

In capitalist countries, where the Communist Party does not possess any means of coercion, it is obvious that it can give leadership only by Communists being in the trade unions as rank-and-file members or as part of their full-time staff.

The number of Communists in leading posts of the trade unions is only one of the means of measuring the role of the party in the unions. The most important measurement is the percentage of rank-and-file Communists in relation to the whole unionized mass. But the principal criterion is the general influence of the party on the working class, which is measured by the circulation of the Communist press, the attendance at meetings of the party, the number of votes at elections, and, what is especially important, the number of working men and women who respond actively to the party's appeals to struggle.

13. It is clear that the influence of the Communist Party in general will grow, including in the trade unions, the more revolutionary the situation becomes.

These conditions permit an appreciation of the degree and the form of the true, real, and not metaphysical autonomy of the trade unions. In times of "peace," when the most militant forms of trade union action are isolated economic strikes, the *direct* role of the party in trade union action falls back to second place. As a general rule the party does not make a decision on every isolated strike. It *helps* the trade union to decide if the strike is opportune by means of its political and economic information and by its advice. It *serves* the strike with its agitation, etc. First place in the strike belongs, of course, to the trade union.

The situation changes radically when the movement rises to the general strike and still more to the direct struggle for power. In these conditions the leading role of the party becomes entirely direct, open, and immediate. The trade unions—naturally not those that pass over to the other side of the barricades—become the organizational apparatus of the party, which, in the presence of the whole class, stands forth as the leader of the revolution, bearing the full responsibility.

In the field extending between the partial economic strike and the revolutionary class insurrection are placed all the possible forms of reciprocal relations between the party and the trade unions, the varying degrees of direct and immediate leadership, and so forth.

But under all conditions the party seeks to win general leadership by relying upon the real autonomy of the trade unions, which, as organizations—it goes without saying—do not "submit" to it.

Political independence of the unions is a myth

14. Facts show that politically "independent" unions do not exist anywhere. There never have been any. Experience and

theory say that there never will be any. In the United States the trade unions are directly bound by their apparatus to the general staffs of industry and the bourgeois parties. In Britain the trade unions, which in the past mainly supported the Liberals, now constitute the material basis of the Labour Party. In Germany the trade unions march under the banner of the Social Democracy. In the Soviet republic their leadership belongs to the Bolsheviks. In France one of the trade union organizations follows the Socialists, the other the Communists. In Finland the trade unions divided only a little while ago, one going toward the Social Democracy, the other toward communism. That is how it is everywhere.

The theoreticians of the "independence" of the trade union movement have not taken the trouble up to now to think out this question: Why their slogan not only does not approach its realization in practice anywhere, but why, on the contrary, the dependence of the trade unions upon the leadership of a party becomes everywhere, without exception, more and more evident and open. Yet this corresponds entirely to the character of the imperialist epoch, which bares all class relations and which, even within the proletariat, accentuates the contradictions between its aristocracy and its most exploited sections.

The Syndicalist League—embryo of a party

15. The consummate expression of outdated syndicalism is the so-called Syndicalist League. By all its traits it comes forward as a political organization that seeks to subordinate the trade union movement to its influence. In fact the league recruits its members not in accordance with the trade union principle but in accordance with the principle of political groupings; it has its platform, if not its program, and it defends it in its publications; it has its own internal discipline within the trade union movement. In the congresses of the confederations its partisans act as a political fraction in the same way as the Communist fraction. If we are not to lose ourselves in words, the tendency of the Syndicalist League reduces itself to a struggle

to liberate the two confederations from the leadership of the Socialists and Communists and to unite them under the direction of the Monatte group.

The [Syndicalist] League does not act openly in the name of the right and the necessity for the advanced minority to fight to extend its influence over the most backward masses; it presents itself masked by what it calls trade union "independence." From this point of view, the league resembles the Socialist Party, which also realizes its leadership under cover of the phrase "independence of the trade union movement." The Communist Party, on the contrary, says openly to the working class: Here is my program, my tactics, and my policy, which I propose to the trade unions.

The proletariat must never believe anything blindly. It must judge every party and every organization by its work. But the workers should have a double and triple distrust toward those pretenders to leadership who act incognito, under a mask, who make the proletariat believe that it has no need of leadership in general.

The proletariat demands not that the unions be autonomous, but that they provide correct leadership

16. The right of a political party to fight to win the trade unions to its influence must not be denied, but this question must be posed: In the name of what program and what tactics is this organization fighting? From this point of view the Syndicalist League does not give the necessary guarantees. Its program is extremely amorphous as are its tactics. In its political evaluations it acts only from event to event. Acknowledging the proletarian revolution and even the dictatorship of the proletariat, it ignores the party and fights against Communist leadership, without which the proletarian revolution would always risk remaining an empty phrase.

17. The ideology of trade union independence has nothing in common with the ideas and sentiments of the proletariat as a class. If the party, by its leadership, is capable of assuring a

correct, clear-sighted, and firm policy in the trade unions, not a single worker will have the idea of rebelling against the leadership of the party. The historical experience of the Bolsheviks has proved that.

This also holds good for France, where the Communists received 1.2 million votes in the elections while the Unitary General Confederation of Labor, the central organization of the Red trade unions, has only a fourth or a third of this number. It is clear that the abstract slogan of independence can in no way come from the masses. Trade union bureaucracy is quite another thing. It not only sees in the party bureaucracy professional competition, but it even tends to make itself independent of control by the vanguard of the proletariat. The slogan of independence is, by its very basis, a bureaucratic and not a class slogan.

The fetish of trade union unity

18. After the fetish of "independence" the Syndicalist League also transforms the question of *trade union unity* into a fetish.

It goes without saying that the maintenance of the unity of the trade union organizations has enormous advantages from the point of view of the daily tasks of the proletariat, as well as from the point of view of the struggle of the Communist Party to extend its influence over the masses. But the facts prove that since the first successes of the revolutionary wing in the trade unions, the opportunists have set themselves deliberately on the road of split. Peaceful relations with the bourgeoisie are dearer to them than the unity of the proletariat. That is the indubitable summary of the postwar experience.

We Communists are in every way interested in proving to the workers that the responsibility for splitting the trade union organizations falls wholly upon the Social Democracy. But it does not at all follow that the hollow formula of unity is more important for us than the revolutionary tasks of the working class.

19. Eight years have passed since the trade union split in

France. During this time the two organizations linked themselves definitely with the two mortally hostile political parties. Under these conditions, to think of being able to unify the trade union movement by the simple preaching of unity would be to nurture illusions. To declare that without the preliminary unification of the two trade union organizations not only the proletarian revolution but even a serious class struggle is impossible means to make the future of the revolution depend upon the corrupted clique of trade union reformists.

In fact, the future of the revolution depends not upon the fusion of the two trade union apparatuses but upon the unification of the majority of the working class around revolutionary slogans and revolutionary methods of struggle.

At present the unification of the working class is possible only by fighting against the class collaborationists (coalitionists) who are found not only in political parties but also in the trade unions.

20. The real road to the revolutionary unity of the proletariat lies in the development, the correction, the enlargement, and the consolidation of the revolutionary CGTU and in the weakening of the reformist CGT.

It is not excluded but, on the contrary, very likely that at the time of its revolution the French proletariat will enter the struggle with two confederations: behind one will be found the masses and behind the other, the aristocracy of labor and the bureaucracy.

Nature of the trade union opposition

21. The new trade union opposition obviously does not want to enter on the road of syndicalism. At the same time it breaks with the party—not with a certain leadership but with the party in general. This means quite simply that ideologically it definitely disarms itself and falls back to the positions of craft or trade unionism.

22. The trade union opposition as a whole is quite variegated. But it is characterized by some common features that do

not bring it closer to the Left Communist Opposition but, on the contrary, estrange it from and counterpose it to the Left Opposition.

The trade union opposition does not fight against the thoughtless acts and wrong methods of the Communist leadership, but against the influence of communism over the working class.

The trade union opposition does not fight against the ultraleftist evaluation of the given situation and the tempo of its development but acts, in reality, counter to revolutionary perspectives in general.

The trade union opposition does not fight against caricatured methods of antimilitarism but puts forward a pacifist orientation. In other words, the trade union opposition is manifestly developing in the reformist spirit.

23. It is entirely wrong to affirm that in these recent years—contrary to what has happened in Germany, Czechoslovakia, and other countries—there has not been constituted in France a right-wing grouping in the revolutionary camp. The main point is that, forsaking the revolutionary policy of communism, the Right Opposition in France, in conformity with the traditions of the French labor movement, has assumed a trade union character, concealing in this way its political physiognomy. At bottom, the majority of the trade union opposition represents the right wing, just as does the Brandler group in Germany, the Czech trade unionists who after the split have taken a clearly reformist position, etc.

Policy of the Communist Party

24. One may seek to object that all the preceding considerations would be correct only on condition that the Communist Party has a correct policy. But this objection is unfounded. The question of the relationship between the party, which represents the proletariat as it should be, and the trade unions, which represent the proletariat as it is, is the most fundamental question of revolutionary Marxism. It would be veritable suicide to

spurn the only possible principled reply to this question solely because the Communist Party, under the influence of objective and subjective reasons of which we have spoken more than once, is now conducting a false policy toward the trade unions, as well as in other fields. A correct policy must be counterposed to a wrong policy. Toward this end, the Left Opposition has been constituted as a faction. If it is considered that the French Communist Party in its entirety is in a wholly irremediable or hopeless state—which we absolutely do not think—then another party must be counterposed to it.

But the question of the relation of the party to the class does not change one iota because of this fact. The Left Opposition considers that to influence the trade union movement, to help it find its correct orientation, to permeate it with correct slogans, is impossible except through the Communist Party (or a faction for the moment) which, besides its other attributes, is the central ideological laboratory of the working class.

25. The task of the Communist Party, correctly understood, does not consist solely of gaining influence over the trade unions, such as they are, but of winning, through the trade unions, influence over the majority of the working class. This is possible only if the methods employed by the party in the trade unions correspond to the nature and the tasks of the latter. The struggle of the party for influence in the trade unions finds its objective verification in whether they do or do not thrive, and in whether the number of their members increases, as well as in their relations with the broadest masses. If the party buys its influence in the trade unions only at the price of a narrowing down and a factionalizing of the latter—converting them into auxiliaries of the party for momentary aims and preventing them from becoming genuine mass organizations—then the relations between the party and the class are wrong. It is not necessary for us to dwell here on the causes for such a situation. We have done it more than once and we do it every day. The changeability of the official Communist policy reflects its adventurist tendency to make itself master of the working class

in the briefest time, by means of stage play, inventions, superficial agitation, and so forth.

The way out of this situation does not, however, lie in counterposing the trade unions to the party (or to the faction) but in the irreconcilable struggle to change the whole policy of the party as well as that of the trade unions.

Tasks of the Communist left

26. The Left Opposition must place the questions of the trade union movement in indissoluble connection with the questions of the political struggle of the proletariat. It must give a concrete analysis of the present stage of development of the French labor movement. It must give an evaluation, quantitative as well as qualitative, of the present strike movement and its perspectives in relation to the perspectives of the economic development of France.

Needless to say, it completely rejects the perspective of decades of capitalist stabilization and pacifism. It proceeds from an estimation of our epoch as a revolutionary one. It starts from the necessity of a timely preparation of the proletarian vanguard in face of the abrupt turns that are not only probable but inevitable. The firmer and more implacable is its action against the supposedly revolutionary rantings of the centrist bureaucracy,[26] against political hysteria that does not take conditions into account and confuses today with yesterday or with tomorrow, the more firmly and resolutely must it set itself against the elements of the right that take up its criticism and conceal themselves under it in order to introduce their tendencies into revolutionary Marxism.

※

27. A new definition of boundaries? New polemics? New splits? That will be the lament of the good but tired souls who would like to transform the Opposition into a calm retreat where one can tranquilly rest from the great tasks, while preserving

intact the name of revolutionist "of the left." No! We say to them, to these tired souls: We are certainly not traveling the same road. Truth has never yet been the sum of small errors. A revolutionary organization has never yet been composed of small conservative groups seeking primarily to distinguish themselves from each other. There are epochs when the revolutionary tendency is reduced to a small minority in the labor movement. But these epochs demand not arrangements between the small groups with mutual hiding of sins but, on the contrary, a doubly implacable struggle for a correct perspective and an education of the cadres in the spirit of genuine Marxism. Victory is possible only in this way.

28. So far as the author of these lines is personally concerned, he must admit that the notion he had of the Monatte group when he was deported from the Soviet Union proved to be too optimistic and, by that fact, false. For many years the author did not have the possibility of following the activity of this group. He judged it from old memories. The divergences showed themselves in fact not only more profound but even more acute than one might have supposed. The events of recent times have proved beyond a doubt that without a clear and precise ideological demarcation from the line of syndicalism the Communist Opposition in France will not go forward. The theses proposed here represent by themselves the first step on the road of this demarcation, which is the prelude to the successful struggle against the revolutionary jabberings and the opportunist essence of Cachin, Monmousseau, and company.

The errors in principle of syndicalism

A contribution to the discussion with Monatte and his friends

When I arrived in France in October 1914, I found the French Socialist and trade union movement in a state of the deepest chauvinist demoralization. In the search for revolutionists, with candle in hand, I made the acquaintance of Monatte and Rosmer. They had not succumbed to chauvinism. It was thus that our friendship began. Monatte considered himself an anarcho-syndicalist; despite that, he was immeasurably closer to me than were the French Guesdists, who were playing a pitiful and shameful role.[27] At that time the Cachins were familiarizing themselves with the servants' entrance to the ministries of the [French] Third Republic and the Allied embassies. In 1915 Monatte left the central committee of the CGT, slamming the door behind him. His departure from the trade union center was in essence nothing else but a split. At that time, however, Monatte believed, and rightly so, that the fundamental historic tasks of the proletariat stood above unity with chauvinists and lackeys of imperialism. It was in this that Monatte was loyal to the best traditions of revolutionary syndicalism.

Monatte was one of the first friends of the October revolution. True, unlike Rosmer he had held aloof for a long time. That was well in keeping with the character of Monatte, as I was later convinced, of standing aside, of waiting, of criticizing. At times this is absolutely unavoidable. But as a *basic* line of conduct it becomes a kind of sectarianism that has a close affinity to Proudhonism but nothing in common with Marxism.

When the Socialist Party of France became the Communist Party, I frequently had occasion to discuss with Lenin the onerous heritage the International had received in the person of leaders like Cachin, Frossard, and other heroes of the League of the Rights of Man, of the Freemasons, of parliamentarians, careerists, and babblers. One of these conversations—if I am not mistaken I have already published it in the press—follows:

"It would be good," Lenin said to me, "to drive out all these weathercocks, and to draw into the party the revolutionary syndicalists, the militant workers, people who are really devoted to the cause of the working class. And Monatte?"

"Monatte would of course be ten times better than Cachin and those like him," I replied. "But Monatte not only continues to reject parliamentarism but to this day he has not grasped the significance of the party."

Lenin was astonished: "Impossible! Has not grasped the significance of the party after the October revolution? That's a very disturbing symptom."

I carried on a correspondence with Monatte in which I invited him to Moscow. He was evasive. True to his nature, he preferred in this case, too, to stand aside and wait. And besides, the Communist Party did not suit him. In that he was right. But instead of helping to transform it, he waited. At the Fourth Congress [of the Communist International] we succeeded in taking the first step toward cleansing the Communist Party of France of Freemasons, pacifists, and office-seekers. Monatte entered the party. But it is not necessary to emphasize the fact that this did not mean to us that he had adopted the Marxian viewpoint; not at all.

On March 23, 1923, I wrote in *Pravda:* "The entrance of our old friend Monatte into the Communist Party was a great day for us. The revolution needs men of this kind. But it would be wrong to pay for a rapprochement with a confusion of ideas."[28] In this article, I criticized the scholasticism of Louzon on the relations between the class, the trade unions, and the party. In particular I explained that prewar syndicalism had been an embryo of the Communist Party, that this embryo had since become a child, and that if this child was suffering from measles and rickets it was necessary to nourish and cure it, but that it would be absurd to imagine that it could be made to return to its mother's womb. I may perhaps be permitted to say in this regard that the arguments of my 1923 article, in caricature, serve to this day as the main weapons against Monatte in the hands of Monmousseau and other anti-Trotskyist warriors.

Monatte joined the party; but he hardly had time to turn about and accustom himself to a house far vaster than his little shop on the Quai de Jemmapes when the coup d'état in the International burst upon him: Lenin was taken ill, the campaign against "Trotskyism" began, as did the Zinovievist "Bolshevization."[29] Monatte could not submit to the careerists who, by leaning on the general staff of the epigones at Moscow and disposing of unlimited resources, carried on by means of intrigue and slander.

Monatte was expelled from the party. This episode, important but still only an episode, was of decisive importance in the political development of Monatte. He decided that his brief experience in the party had fully confirmed his anarcho-syndicalist prejudices against the party in general. Monatte then began insistently to retrace his steps toward abandoned positions. He began to seek again the Charter of Amiens. To do all that, he had to turn his face to the past. The experiences of the war, of the Russian revolution, and of the world trade union movement were lost upon him, leaving hardly a trace. Once again Monatte stood aside and waited. What for? A new Amiens congress. During the last few years I was unfortunately unable to follow the retrogressive evolution of Monatte—the Russian Opposition lived in a blockaded circle.

Out of the whole treasure of the theory and practice of the world struggle of the proletariat, Monatte has extracted but two ideas: *trade union autonomy* and *trade union unity*. He has elevated these two pure principles above sinful reality. It is on trade union autonomy and trade union unity that he has based his newspaper and his Syndicalist League. Unfortunately, these two ideas are hollow and each of them resembles the hole in a ring. Whether the ring be made of iron, silver, or gold, Monatte does not care in the least. The ring, you see, always hampers the trade unions' activity. Monatte is interested only in the hole of autonomy.

No less empty is the other sacred principle: *unity*. In its name Monatte even stood out against the rupture of the Anglo-Russian Committee, even though the General Council of the British trade unions had betrayed the [1926] general strike. The fact that Stalin, Bukharin, Cachin, Monmousseau, and others supported the bloc with the strikebreakers until the latter kicked them out does not in the least reduce Monatte's mistake. After my arrival abroad, I made an attempt to explain to the readers of *La Révolution Prolétarienne* the criminal character of this bloc, the consequences of which are still being felt by the workers' movement. Monatte did not want to publish my article. And how could it have been otherwise, since I had made an assault upon the sacred trade union unity, which solves all questions and reconciles all contradictions.

When strikers encounter a group of strikebreakers in their path, they throw them out of their midst without sparing blows. If the strikebreakers are union men, they throw them out immediately without worrying about the sacred principle of trade union unity. Monatte surely has no objections to this. But the matter is entirely different when it is a question of the trade union bureaucracy and its leaders. The General Council is not composed of starving and backward strikebreakers; no, they are well-fed and experienced traitors who found it necessary at a given moment to stand at the head of the general strike in order to decapitate it all the more quickly and surely. They worked hand in hand with the government, the bosses, and the church. It would seem that the leaders of the Russian trade unions, who were in a political bloc with the General Council, should have immediately, openly, and relentlessly broken with it at that very moment, in full view of the masses deceived and betrayed by it. But Monatte rises up fiercely: it is forbidden to disturb trade union unity. In an astonishing manner he forgets that he himself upset this unity in 1915 by leaving the chauvinist general council of the General Confederation of Labor.

It must be said outright: between the Monatte of 1915 and the Monatte of 1929 there is an abyss. To Monatte it seems that he is remaining entirely faithful to himself. Formally this is true, up to a certain point. Monatte repeats a few old formulas, but he ignores entirely the experiences of the last fifteen years, richer in lessons than all the preceding history of humanity. In the attempt to return to his former positions, Monatte fails to notice that they disappeared a long time ago. No matter what question is raised, Monatte looks backward. This may be seen most clearly in the question of the party and the state.

Some time ago Monatte accused me of underrating the "dangers" of state power (*La Révolution Prolétarienne*, no. 79, May 1, 1929, p. 2). This reproach is not a new one; it has its origin in the struggle of Bakunin against Marx and it shows a false, contradictory, and essentially nonproletarian conception of the state.

With the exception of one country, state power throughout the world is in the hands of the bourgeoisie. *It is in this, and only in this, from the point of view of the proletariat, that the danger of state power lies.* The proletariat's historic task is to wrest this most powerful instrument of oppression from the hands of the bourgeoisie. The Communists do not deny the difficulties, the dangers that are connected with the dictatorship of the proletariat. But can this lessen by one iota the necessity to seize power? If the whole proletariat were carried by an irresistible force to the conquest of power, or if it had already conquered it, one could, strictly speaking, understand this or that warning of the syndicalists. Lenin, as is known, warned in his testament against the abuse of revolutionary power.[30] The struggle against the distortions of the dictatorship of the proletariat has been conducted by the Opposition since its inception and without the need of borrowing from the arsenal of anarchism.

But in the bourgeois countries, the misfortune lies in the fact that the overwhelming majority of the proletariat does not understand as it should the dangers of the *bourgeois* state. By the manner in which they treat the question, the syndicalists—unwittingly of course—contribute to the passive conciliation of the workers with the capitalist state. When the syndicalists keep drumming into the workers, who are oppressed by the bourgeois state, their warnings about the dangers of a proletarian state, they play a purely reactionary role. The bourgeois will readily repeat to the workers, "Do not touch the state because it is a snare full of dangers to you." The Communist will say to the workers, "As for the difficulties and dangers with which the proletariat is confronted the day after the conquest of power—we will learn to overcome them on the basis of experience. But at the present time, the most menacing dangers lie in the fact that our class enemy holds the reins of power in its hands and directs it against us."

In contemporary society there are only two classes capable of holding power in their hands: the capitalist bourgeoisie and the revolutionary proletariat. The petty bourgeoisie long ago lost the economic possibility of directing the destinies of modern society. Now and then, in fits of desperation, it rises for the conquest of power, even with arms in hand, as has happened in Italy, in Poland, and in other countries. But the fascist insurrections only end in this result: the new power becomes the instrument of finance capital under an even more naked and brutal form. That is why the most representative ideologists of the petty bourgeoisie are afraid of state power as such. The petty bourgeoisie fears power when it is in the hands of the big bourgeoisie, because the latter strangles and ruins it. The petty bourgeoisie also fears power when it is in the hands of the proletariat, for the latter undermines all the conditions of its habitual existence. Finally, it fears power when it falls into its own hands because it must inevitably pass out of its impotent hands into those of finance capital or the proletariat. The anarchists do not see the revolutionary problems of state power, its historical role, and see only the "dangers" of state power. The antistate anarchists are consequently the most logical and, for that reason, the most hopeless representatives of the petty bourgeoisie in its historical blind alley.

Yes, the dangers of state power exist under the regime of the dictatorship of the proletariat as well, but the substance of these dangers consists in the fact that power can actually return to the hands of the bourgeoisie. The best known and most obvious state danger is bureaucratism. But what is its essence? If the enlightened workers' bureaucracy could lead society to socialism, that is, to the liquidation of the state, we would be reconciled to such a bureaucracy. But it has an entirely opposite character: by separating itself from the proletariat, by raising itself above it, the bureaucracy falls under the influence of the petty-bourgeois classes and can by that very fact facilitate the return of power into the hands of the bourgeoisie. In other words, the dangers of the state for the workers under the dictatorship of the proletariat are, in the final analysis, nothing but the danger of restoring the power to the bourgeoisie.

The question of the *source* of this bureaucratic danger is no less important. It would be radically wrong to think, to imagine, that bureaucratism rises exclusively from the fact of the conquest of power by the proletariat. No, that is not the case. In the capitalist states the most monstrous forms of bureaucratism are to be observed precisely in the trade unions. It is enough to look at the United States, Britain, and Germany. The Amsterdam International is the most powerful international organization of the trade union bureaucracy. It is thanks to it that the whole structure of capitalism now stands upright, above all in Europe and especially in Britain.

If there were not a bureaucracy of the trade unions, then the police, the army, the courts, the lords, the monarchy would appear before the proletarian masses as nothing but pitiful and ridiculous playthings. The bureaucracy of the trade unions is the backbone of British imperialism. It is by means of this bureaucracy that the bourgeoisie exists, not only in the metropolis but in India, in Egypt, and in the other colonies.

One would have to be completely blind to say to the British workers, "Be on guard against the conquest of power and always remember that your trade unions are the antidote to the dangers of the state." The Marxist will say to the British workers, "The trade union bureaucracy is the chief instrument for your oppression by the bourgeois state. Power must be wrested from the hands of the bourgeoisie, and for that its principal agent, the trade union bureaucracy, must be overthrown." Parenthetically, it is especially for this reason that the bloc of Stalin with the strikebreakers was so criminal.

From the example of Britain one sees very clearly how absurd it is to counterpose, as if it were a question of two different principles, the trade union organization and the state organization. In Britain more than anywhere else the state rests upon the back of the working class, which constitutes the overwhelming majority of the population of the country. The mechanism is such that the bureaucracy is based *directly* on the workers, and the state indirectly, *through the intermediary* of the trade union bureaucracy.

Up to now, we have not mentioned the Labour Party, which in Britain, the classical country of trade unions, is only a political transposition of the same trade union bureaucracy. The same leaders guide the trade unions, betray the general strike, lead the electoral campaign, and later on sit in the ministries. The Labour Party and the trade unions—these are not two principles; they are only a technical division of labor. Together they are the fundamental support of the domination of the British bourgeoisie. The latter cannot be overthrown without overthrowing the Labourite bureaucracy. And that cannot be attained by counterposing the trade union as such to the state as such, but only by the active opposition of the Communist Party to the Labourite bureaucracy in all fields of social life: in the trade unions, in strikes, in the electoral campaign, in Parliament, and in power. The principal task of a real party of the proletariat consists in putting itself at the head of the working masses, organized in trade unions and unorganized, to wrest power from the bourgeoisie and to strike a deathblow to the "dangers of statism."

Monatte crosses the Rubicon

In late 1930 forces close to Pierre Monatte initiated a declaration calling for trade union unity on the basis of the 1906 syndicalist Charter of Amiens, the class struggle, and independence "without any interference from political parties, factions, and sects." The statement was signed by twenty-two unionists from both the CGTU and CGT.

Among the signers was CGT official Georges Dumoulin. During the early stages of World War I, Dumoulin and Alphonse Merrheim had led opposition in the CGT to its leadership's chauvinist stand. In 1917, however, as mass opposition to the war mounted, the CGT majority leadership responded by voicing criticisms of the government's war policy. Merrheim and Dumoulin then formed a bloc with the CGT's top officials in support of a negotiated peace and of the war aims voiced by U.S. President Woodrow Wilson.

It is now ridiculous and out of place to speak of joint action with the Syndicalist League or the Committee for Trade Union Independence. Monatte has crossed the Rubicon. He has lined up with Dumoulin against communism, against the October revolution, against the proletarian revolution in general. For

Dumoulin belongs to the camp of the especially dangerous and perfidious enemies of the proletarian revolution. He has demonstrated this in action, in the most repugnant manner. For a long time he has prowled around the left wing only to rally at the decisive moment to Jouhaux, that is, to the most servile and most corrupt agent of capital.

The task of the honest revolutionist—above all in France, where unpunished betrayals are innumerable—consists in reminding the workers of the experiences of the past, of tempering the youth in intransigence, of recounting tirelessly the history of the betrayal of the Second International and of French syndicalism, of unmasking the shameful role played not only by Jouhaux and company but above all by the French syndicalists of the "left" like Merrheim and Dumoulin. Whoever does not carry out this elementary duty to the new generation deprives himself forever of the right to revolutionary confidence. Can one, for instance, preserve a shadow of esteem for the toothless French anarchists when they again play up as an "antimilitarist" the old buffoon Sébastien Faure, who trafficked with pacifist phrases in peacetime and flung himself into the arms of Malvy, that is, of the French stock exchange, at the beginning of the war?[31] Whoever seeks to drape these facts in the toga of oblivion, whoever grants amnesty to political traitors, can only be considered by us an incorrigible enemy.

Monatte has crossed the Rubicon. From the uncertain ally, he has become first the hesitant foe in order to become, later on, the direct enemy. We must say this to the workers clearly, aloud, and unsparingly.

To simple people, and also to some knaves who put on a simple air, our judgment may appear exaggerated and "unjust." For Monatte is uniting with Dumoulin *solely* for the reestablishment of the unity of the trade union movement! Solely! The trade unions, you see, are not a party or a "sect." The trade unions, you see, must embrace the whole working class, all its tendencies. One can therefore work in the trade union field by Dumoulin's side without taking responsibility either for his past or for his future. Reflections of this sort constitute a chain of those cheap sophisms with which the French syndicalists and Socialists love to juggle when they want to cover up a somewhat odorous job.

If united trade unions existed in France, the revolutionists would obviously not have left them just because of the presence of traitors, turncoats, and licensed agents of imperialism. The revolutionists would not have taken upon themselves the initiative for the split. But in joining or in remaining in these trade unions, they would have directed all their efforts to unmasking the traitors before the masses as traitors, in order to discredit them on the basis of the experience of the masses, to isolate them, to deprive them of the confidence they enjoy, and in the end, to help the masses run them out. That alone can justify the participation of revolutionists in the reformist trade unions.

But Monatte does not at all work side by side with Dumoulin within the trade unions as the Bolsheviks frequently had to with the Mensheviks, all the while conducting a systematic struggle against them. No, *Monatte has united with Dumoulin as an ally* on a common platform, creating with him a political faction or "sect" that speaks the language of French syndicalism in order to launch a political crusade for the conquest of the trade union movement. Monatte does not fight against the traitors on the trade union field; on the contrary, he has associated himself with Dumoulin and takes him under his wing, presenting himself to the masses as Dumoulin's tutor. Monatte says to the workers that one can go hand in hand with Dumoulin against the Communists, against the Red International of Labor Unions, against the October revolution, and consequently, against the proletarian revolution in general. This is the unvarnished truth that we must speak aloud to the workers.

When we once defined Monatte as *a centrist slipping toward the right,* Chambelland sought to transform this entirely correct scientific definition into a feuilleton joke and even to throw the centrist designation back at us,[32] just as a soccer player

returns the ball by hitting it with his head. Alas, the head sometimes suffers for it! Yes, Monatte was a centrist, and in his centrism were contained all the elements of his manifest opportunism of today.

Apropos of the execution of the Indochinese revolutionists
in the spring of this year,[33] Monatte developed the following
plan of action, in an indirect manner:

"I do not understand why, in such circumstances, the parties
and organizations disposing of the necessary means do not send
deputies and journalists to investigate on the very spot. Out of
the dozen deputies of the Communist Party, and out of the
hundred of the Socialist Party, could they not select an investigation commission that would have returned with the materi-
als for a campaign capable of making the colonialists retreat
and of saving the condemned?" (*La Révolution Prolétarienne*,
no. 104.)

With the imperious reproaches of a school monitor, Monatte gave the Communists and the Social Democrats advice
on the manner of fighting against the "colonialists." For him
the social patriots and Communists were people *of the same
camp* six months ago, who had only to follow Monatte's advice
in order to carry out a correct policy. It did not even occur to
Monatte to ask how the social patriots can fight against the
"colonialists" when they are the partisans and the practical ex-
ecutors of the colonial policy. For can colonies, that is, nations,
tribes, races, be governed without shooting down the rebels,
the revolutionists who seek to liberate themselves from the
repulsive colonial yoke? [Socialist Party leader Jean] Zyromsky and his ilk are not opposed to presenting upon every propitious occasion a drawing-room protest against colonial "besti-
ality"; but that does not prevent them from belonging to the
social-colonialist party that harnessed the French proletariat to
a chauvinistic course during the war, one of whose principal
aims was to preserve and extend the colonies to the profit of
the French bourgeoisie.

Monatte has forgotten all this. He reasoned as if there had

not been, after this, great revolutionary events in a number of Western and Eastern countries, as if the various tendencies had not been changed by events and their character had not been revealed by experience. Six months ago Monatte pretended to start all over again. And during this time, history again made game of him. MacDonald, the coreligionist of the French syndicalists, to whom Louzon recently gave some incomparable advice, sends to India not liberating commissions of investigation but armed forces, and deals with the Hindus in a more repulsive manner than would any Curzon. And all the scoundrels of British trade unionism approve this butcher's work. Is this by chance?[34]

Instead of turning away, under the influence of the new lesson, from hypocritical "neutrality" and "independence," Monatte, on the contrary, has taken a new step—this time a decisive one—into the arms of the French MacDonalds and Thomases. We have nothing more to discuss with Monatte.

The bloc of the "independent" syndicalists with the avowed agents of the bourgeoisie has great symptomatic significance. In the eyes of philistines things seem as though the representatives of both camps had taken a step toward each other in the name of unity, of the cessation of the fratricidal struggle, and other sweet phrases. There can be nothing more disgusting, more false, than this phraseology. In reality the meaning of the bloc is entirely different.

In the various circles of the labor bureaucracy and also in part in circles of the workers themselves, Monatte represents those elements who sought to approach the revolution but who lost hope in it through the experience of the last ten or twelve years. It develops by such complicated and perplexing roads, don't you see, that it leads to internal conflicts, to ever new splits, and after a step forward it takes a half step and sometimes a full step backward.

The years of bourgeois stabilization, the years of the ebbing of the revolutionary tide, have heaped up despair, fatigue, and opportunist moods in a certain part of the working class. All these sentiments have only now matured in the Monatte group and have driven it to pass definitively from one camp to the other. On the way, Monatte met with Louis Sellier, who had his own reasons for turning his back, covered with municipal honors, to the revolution. Monatte and Sellier have quit together. To their meeting, there came no less a one than Dumoulin. This means that at the moment when Monatte shifted from left to right, Dumoulin judged it opportune to shift from right to left. How is this to be explained? It is because Monatte, as an empiricist—and centrists are always empiricists, otherwise they would not be centrists—has expressed his sentiments on the period of capitalist stabilization at a moment when this period *has begun to be transformed into another, much less tranquil and much less stable.*

The world crisis has taken on gigantic dimensions and for the moment it is becoming deeper. Nobody can predict where it will stop or what political consequences it will bring in its train. The situation in Germany is extremely strained. The German elections produced acute elements of disturbance, not only in internal relations but also in international relations, showing again on what foundation the edifice of Versailles rests.[35]

The economic crisis has inundated the frontiers of France, and we already see there, after a long interlude, the beginnings of unemployment. During the years of relative prosperity the French workers suffered from the policy of the CGT bureaucracy. During the years of crisis they can remind it of its betrayals and its crimes. Jouhaux cannot but be uneasy. He necessarily requires a left wing, perhaps more necessarily than [Socialist Party leader Léon] Blum. What purpose then does Dumoulin serve? Obviously it must not be thought that everything is arranged like the keys of a piano and has been formulated in a conversation. That is not necessary. All these people know each other; they know what they are capable of and especially the limits to which one of them can go to the left with impunity for himself and his bosses.

The fact that the CGT bureaucracy preserves a watchful and

critical attitude toward Dumoulin, sometimes even with a nuance of hostility, in no way invalidates what is said above. The reformists must take their measures of precaution and keep an eye on Dumoulin so that he does not let himself get carried away by the work with which the reformists have charged him and go beyond the limits marked out.

Dumoulin takes his place in the line of march as the left wing of Jouhaux at the very moment when Monatte, who has shifted constantly to the right, has decided to cross the Rubicon. Dumoulin must reestablish his reputation at least a little—with the aid of Monatte and at his expense. Jouhaux can have no objection when his own Dumoulin compromises Monatte. In this way, everything is in order: Monatte has broken with the left camp at the moment when the CGT bureaucracy has felt the necessity of covering up its uncovered left flank.

We are analyzing personal shifts not for Monatte, who was once our friend, and certainly not for Dumoulin, whom we long ago judged as an irreconcilable enemy. What interests us is the *symptomatic* significance of these personal regroupings, which reflect far more profound processes in the working masses themselves.

This radicalization, which the clamorers proclaimed two years ago, is indisputably approaching today. The economic crisis has arrived in France—after a delay, it is true; it is not impossible that it will unfold in a mild manner compared with Germany. Experience alone can establish this. But it is indisputable that the balanced state of passivity in which the French working class existed in the years of the so-called radicalization will give way in a very brief time to a growing activity and a spirit of militancy. It is toward this new period that the revolutionists must turn.

On the threshold of the new period, Monatte gathers up the fatigued, the disillusioned, the exhausted, and makes them pass into the camp of Jouhaux. So much the worse for Monatte, so much the better for the revolution!

The period opening before us will not be a period of the

growth of the false neutrality of the trade unions but, on the contrary, the period of the reinforcement of communist positions in the labor movement. Great tasks present themselves to the Left Opposition. With sure successes awaiting it, what must it do to gain them? Nothing but *remain faithful to itself.* But on this point next time.

January 4, 1931

The mistakes of rightist elements of the Communist League on the trade union question

Some preliminary remarks

In October 1929 the CGTU Teachers Federation leadership issued a manifesto opposing both the Communist Party leadership of the CGTU and Monatte's syndicalist Committee for Trade Union Independence. At the same time, however, its manifesto indicated that the Communist Party, "despite its faults and weaknesses," remained "the only revolutionary organization of the proletariat." In April 1930 Communist League leaders collaborated with the Teachers Federation leadership in forming the Unitary Opposition in the CGTU.

By the beginning of 1931, however, many in the Communist League had concluded that the Unitary Opposition did not provide a way forward for French trade unions. In this article Trotsky opposed the policy of league trade union work director Pierre Gourget, who argued for continued support to the Unitary Opposition.

1. Whereas the theoretical structure of the political economy of Marxism rests entirely upon the conception of *value* as materialized labor, the revolutionary policy of Marxism rests upon the conception of the *party* as the vanguard of the proletariat.

Whatever may be the social sources and political causes of opportunistic mistakes and deviations, they are always reduced ideologically to an erroneous understanding of the revolutionary party, of its relation to other proletarian organizations and to the class as a whole.

2. The conception of the party as the proletarian vanguard presupposes its full and unconditional independence from all other organizations. The various agreements (blocs, coalitions, compromises) with other organizations, unavoidable in the course of the class struggle, are permissible only on the condition that the party always turns its own face toward the class, always marches under its own banner, acts in its own name, and clearly explains to the masses the aims and limits within which it concludes the given agreement.

3. At the basis of all the oscillations and all the errors of the Comintern leadership, we find the wrong understanding of the nature of the party and its tasks. The Stalinist theory of a "two-class party" contradicts the ABC of Marxism.[36] The fact that the official Communist International has tolerated this theory for a number of years, and to this day has not yet condemned it with the necessary firmness, is the most unmistakable sign of the falsity of its official doctrine.

4. The fundamental crime of the centrist bureaucracy in the USSR is its false position regarding the party. The Stalinist faction seeks to include administratively in the ranks of the party the whole working class. The party ceases to be the vanguard, that is, the voluntary selection of the most advanced, the most conscious, the most devoted, and the most active workers. The party is fused with the class as it is and loses its power of resistance to the bureaucratic apparatus. On the other hand, the Brandlerites and the other hangers-on of the centrist bureaucracy justify the Stalinist party regime by the philistine reference to the "lack of culture" of the Russian proletariat, thus identifying the party and the class, that is, liquidating the party in theory as Stalin liquidates it in practice.

5. The basis of the disastrous policy of the Comintern in

China was the renunciation of the independence of the party. Practical agreements with the Kuomintang were unavoidable in a certain period. The entrance of the Communist Party into the Kuomintang was a fatal error. The development of this mistake was transformed into one of the greatest crimes in history.[37] The Chinese Communist Party was created only in order to transfer its authority to the Kuomintang. From the vanguard of the proletariat, it was transformed into the tail of the bourgeoisie.

6. The disastrous experiment with the Anglo-Russian Committee was based entirely upon trampling underfoot the independence of the British Communist Party. In order that the Soviet trade unions might maintain the bloc with the strikebreakers of the General Council (allegedly in the state interests of the USSR!), the British Communist Party had to be deprived of all independence. This was obtained by the actual dissolution of the party into the so-called Minority Movement, that is, the leftist opposition inside the trade unions.

7. The experience of the Anglo-Russian Committee was unfortunately the least understood and grasped even in the Left Opposition groups. The demand for a break with the strikebreakers[38] appeared even to some within our ranks as sectarianism. Especially with Monatte, the original sin that led him into the arms of Dumoulin was most clearly manifested in the question of the Anglo-Russian Committee. Yet this question has a gigantic importance: without a clear understanding of what happened in Britain in 1925–26, neither communism as a whole nor the Left Opposition in particular will be able to make its way to a broad road.

8. Stalin, Bukharin, Zinoviev—in this question they were all in solidarity, at least initially—sought to replace the weak British Communist Party by a "broader current," which had at its head, to be sure, not members of the party, but "friends," almost-Communists, at any rate fine fellows and good acquaintances. The fine fellows, the "solid leaders," did not, of course, want to submit themselves to the leadership of a small, weak

Communist Party. That was their full right; the party cannot force anybody to submit himself to it. The agreements between the Communists and the "lefts" (Purcell, Hicks, Cook) on the basis of the partial tasks of the trade union movement were, of course, quite possible and in certain cases essential. But on one condition: the Communist Party had to preserve its complete independence, even within the trade unions, act in its own name in all the questions of principle, criticize its "left" allies whenever necessary, and in this way win the confidence of the masses step by step.

This only possible road, however, appeared too long and uncertain to the bureaucrats of the Communist International. They considered that by means of personal influence upon Purcell, Hicks, Cook, and the others (conversations behind the scenes, correspondence, banquets, friendly backslapping, gentle exhortations), they would gradually and imperceptibly draw the leftist opposition ("the broad current") into the bed of the Communist International. To guarantee such a success with greater security, the dear friends (Purcell, Hicks, and Cook) were not to be vexed or exasperated or displeased by petty chicanery, by inopportune criticism, by sectarian intransigence, and so forth. But since one of the tasks of the Communist Party consists precisely in upsetting the peace of and alarming all centrists and semicentrists, a radical measure had to be resorted to by actually subordinating the Communist Party to the Minority Movement. On the trade union field appeared only the leaders of this movement. The British Communist Party had practically ceased to exist for the masses.

9. What did the Russian Left Opposition demand in this question? In the first place, the reestablishment of the complete independence of the British Communist Party in relation to the trade unions. We affirmed that it is only under the influence of the independent slogans of the party and of its open criticism that the Minority Movement could take form, appreciate its tasks more precisely, change its leaders, and fortify itself in the trade unions while consolidating the position of communism.

What did Stalin, Bukharin, Lozovsky, and company reply to our criticism? "You want to push the British Communist Party onto the road of sectarianism. You want to drive Purcell, Hicks, and Cook into the enemy's camp. You want to break with the Minority Movement."

What did the Left Opposition rejoin? "If Purcell and Hicks break with us, not because we demand of them that they transform themselves immediately into Communists—nobody demands that!—but because we ourselves want to remain Communists, this means that Purcell and company are not friends but masked enemies. The quicker they show their real nature the better for the masses. We do not at all want to break with the Minority Movement. On the contrary, we must give the greatest attention to this movement. The smallest step forward with the masses or with a part of the masses is worth more than a dozen abstract programs of circles of intellectuals, but the attention devoted to the masses has nothing in common with capitulation before their temporary leaders and semi-leaders. The masses need a correct orientation and correct slogans. This excludes all theoretical conciliation and all protection of confusionists who exploit the backwardness of the masses."

10. What were the results of Stalin's British experiment? The Minority Movement, embracing almost a million workers, seemed very promising, but it bore the germs of destruction within itself. The masses knew as the leaders of the movement only Purcell, Hicks, and Cook, whom, moreover, Moscow vouched for. These "left" friends, in the first serious test, shamefully betrayed the proletariat. The revolutionary workers were thrown into confusion, sank into apathy, and naturally extended their disappointment to the Communist Party itself, which had been merely the passive part of this whole mechanism of betrayal and perfidy. The Minority Movement was reduced to zero; the Communist Party returned to the existence of a negligible sect. In this way, thanks to a radically false conception of the party, the greatest movement of the British proletariat,

which led to the general strike, not only did not shake the apparatus of the reactionary bureaucracy, but, on the contrary, reinforced it and compromised communism in Great Britain for a long time.

11. One of the psychological sources of opportunism is a superficial impatience, a lack of confidence in the gradual growth of the party's influence, the desire to win the masses by organizational maneuvers or personal diplomacy. Out of this springs the policy of combinations behind the scenes, the policy of silence, of hushing up, of self-renunciation, of adaptation to the ideas and slogans of others; and finally, the complete passage to the positions of opportunism. The subordination of the CP to the Kuomintang in China, the creation of workers' and peasants' parties in India, the subordination of the British party to the Minority Movement, and so on and so forth—in all these phenomena we see the same method of bureaucratic combinationism that commences with a superficial revolutionary impatience and finishes with opportunist treason.*

That is precisely why we have constantly insisted in these last few years upon the enormous educational importance of the examples of the Comintern's strategy cited above. They should be studied and checked all over again at each fresh experience, not only in order to condemn the historical mistakes and crimes after the fact, but to learn to discern similar errors in a new situation at their very inception and consequently while they can still be corrected.

12. It must be said directly: the mistakes of some French

---

* The leading comrades in the United States inform us that in the American [Communist] League certain comrades—to be sure, only individual ones (in the literal sense of the word)—speak for the bloc with the Lovestoneites in the name of "mass work." It is hard to imagine a more ridiculous, a more inept, a more sterile project than this. Do these people know at least a little of the history of the Bolshevik Party? Have they read the works of Lenin? Do they know the correspondence of Marx and Engels? Or has all the history of the revolutionary movement passed them by without leaving a trace? Fortunately, the overwhelming majority of the American league has nothing in common with such ideas.—Leon Trotsky

Oppositionists, members of the league, on the trade union question reveal striking traits of resemblance with the lamentable British experiment. The scale of the errors in France, however, is as yet much smaller, and they have not developed on the basis of a mass movement. This permits certain comrades to overlook these mistakes or to underestimate their importance in principle. Nevertheless, should the league similarly permit its trade union work to be carried on in the future by the methods formulated by the majority of the old leadership, the ideas and the banner of the Left Opposition would be compromised in France for a long time to come.

It would have been criminal to close one's eyes to this. Since there has been no success in rectifying these errors in their initial stage by means of private advice and warnings, then there remains only to name these errors and their authors openly in order to rectify the policy through collective efforts.

13. Beginning in April 1930 the league in effect gave up independent work in the trade unions in order to build the Unitary Opposition, which, for its part, strives to have its own platform, its leadership, its policy. Within these limits we have a striking analogy with the experiment of the Minority Movement in Britain. It must be said, however, that in the French circumstances there are certain features that, from the very beginning, render this experiment even more dangerous. In Britain the Minority Movement as a whole was *more to the left* than the official leadership of the trade unions. Can this be said of the Unitary Opposition? No. In the ranks of the latter there are elements who are obviously tending toward the Right Opposition, that is, toward reformism. Their specific weight is not as yet clear to us.

The principal force of the Unitary Opposition is the Teachers Federation. In France the teachers have always played a serious role in socialism, in syndicalism, and in communism. Among the teachers we shall no doubt find many friends. Nevertheless, the federation as a whole is not a proletarian federation. Because of its social composition the Teachers Federation can furnish very good agitators, journalists, and individual revolutionists, but it cannot become the basis of a trade union movement. All its documents bespeak an insufficient clarity of political thought. The Marseilles congress of the federation demonstrated that its members oscillate in a triangle between the official [Communist Party] course, the Left Opposition, and the Right Opposition. We would render the worst service to the members of the federation, as well as to the whole proletarian movement, if we were to cover up their mistakes, their vacillations, their lack of precision. Unfortunately, up to a few days ago this was the policy of the editorial board of *La Vérité*, a policy of silence, and this was not by chance.

14. "Then you want to break with the Unitary Opposition?" Whoever poses the question this way says by this alone that the Communists, *as Communists*, cannot participate in the work of the Unitary Opposition. But if this were the case it would signify quite simply that the Unitary Opposition is an organization of the masked enemies of communism. Happily, this is not so. The Unitary Opposition as a whole is neither a communist nor an anticommunist organization, because it is *heterogeneous*. We are obliged to take this heterogeneity into account in our practical activity. We can and must display the greatest attention toward groups and even toward individuals that are developing toward Marxism. But all this on one condition: that when we appear before the workers in the trade unions, we act in the name of the Communist League without admitting any censorship of our acts except the control of the league itself (or the whole party after the reestablishment of the unity of the Communist ranks).

15. In the ranks of the Unitary Opposition there are indisputably elements who sympathize strongly with the Left Opposition without being members of the league; they must be brought together under our banner. There are indefinite elements who strive with all their strength to remain in this position, transforming it into a "platform." With these elements we can have tactical agreements on a definite basis, preserving

full freedom of mutual criticism. Finally, in the ranks of the Unitary Opposition there are also, indisputably, alien elements who strayed there accidentally or who penetrated it as recruiting agents of reformism. They make use of obscurity in order to bring about the Unitary Opposition's decomposition. The sooner they are unmasked and eliminated, the better it will be for the cause.

16. But aren't we for collaboration with all workers in the trade unions, regardless of their political and philosophical views? Certainly, but the Unitary Opposition is not a trade union organization; it is a political faction having as its task to influence the trade union movement. Let us leave it to Monatte and his friends the POPists to act under a mask.[39] Revolutionists act openly before the workers. In the Unitary Opposition we can work only with those who go side by side with us, in the same direction, even though not to the end of our road.

17. Certain comrades insist above all that the Communists must fight for their influence on the trade unions by means of ideas and not by mechanical means. This thought, which may seem incontestable, is frequently converted into an empty commonplace. The centrist bureaucracy also declares quite frequently, and quite sincerely, that its task is to influence by ideas and not to exercise a mechanical pressure.

The whole question, in the last analysis, is reduced to the political and economic orientation, to the slogans and the program of action. If the orientation is right, if the slogans correspond to the needs of the moment, then the masses in the trade unions experience no "constraint." On the contrary, if the orientation is wrong, if the policy of revolutionary ascent is proclaimed in a time of political ebb, and conversely, then the mass inevitably perceives this as a mechanical pressure upon it. The question consequently is reduced to whether the theoretical premises of the Left Opposition are sufficiently serious and profound, if its cadres are sufficiently educated to evaluate the situation correctly and to advance the corresponding slogans. All this must be tested in practice. It is therefore all the more impermissible for us to pass over in silence or to underestimate the sins and the mistakes of our temporary allies as well as of ourselves.

18. Certain members of the league, incredible as it may seem, protest against the intention of somebody or other to subordinate the Unitary Opposition to the league.

Without realizing it, they base themselves on the same wretched argument that Monatte uses against communism as a whole. In practice, it means that some comrades working in the trade unions want full independence from the league *for themselves;* they think that by their maneuvers, admonitions, and their personal tact they will achieve results that the league cannot attain by collective work. Other comrades, who would like a similar independence for themselves in the press, welcome these tendencies. The question arises: Why did these comrades join the league if they have no confidence in it?

19. How do matters really stand in regard to the "subordination" of the Unitary Opposition? The very question is false. Only the league's own members are subordinated to it. As long as the majority of the Unitary Opposition is not in the league, it is a question only of persuasion, compromise, or bloc, but certainly not subordination. In fact, the opponents of the so-called subordination of the Unitary Opposition to the league are demanding the effective subordination of the league to the Unitary Opposition. This was precisely the situation until today. In its trade union work, that is, in its most important work, the league is subordinated to the Unitary Opposition, for whose benefit it has renounced all independence. Marxists cannot and must not tolerate such a policy—not even for one more day.

20. Certain leading comrades, who obstinately conducted a policy of capitulation up to yesterday, declare today that they are "completely in agreement" on the necessity of transforming the Unitary Opposition into a bloc. In reality they want to content themselves with a change of name. The quicker they "agree" with the Marxist criticism, the more they conduct, in actuality, a struggle for everything to remain as before. They

simply want to utilize the phraseology of Marxist criticism in order to cover up the old policy. These methods are not new, but time does not render them more attractive. A revolutionary organization would be corrupted for a long time, if not forever, by the poison of duplicity and falsehood if it permitted an opportunist policy to mask itself with revolutionary phraseology. Let us firmly hope that the league will not permit this.

Notes

1. The Sheffield conference, held July 17–21, 1866, brought together 138 delegates representing 200,000 organized workers in Britain. From 1865 to 1867, British unions helped lead a broad campaign for expanded voting rights. In early 1861, following moves by the southern slave states to secede from the United States, unions in cities throughout the northern and border states held meetings and demonstrations supporting the federal government and urging its defense. During the 1861–65 Civil War, new unions were organized and union activity for the eight-hour day increased.

2. Bonapartism refers to a type of class rule that is dictatorial in form and is usually headed by an individual appearing as a "strong man." Originating in a period of social crisis or stalemate of contending class forces, a Bonapartist regime tends to elevate itself above the country's classes and acquire a certain independence of action. The term originates from the regime of Louis-Napoléon Bonaparte in France, 1852–70.

3. This program, entitled "The Death Agony of Capitalism and the Tasks of the Fourth International," is included in Leon Trotsky, *The Transitional Program for Socialist Revolution* (New York: Pathfinder, 1977). The section of this program taking up work in the trade unions appears elsewhere in part 1 of the present collection.

4. The Minority Movement in Britain, the situation in the French trade unions, and developments in the U.S. and Dutch unions referred to in subsequent paragraphs are taken up by Trotsky in other articles in part 1 of this book.

5. In 1937 and 1938 the Mexican government nationalized the railroads and the oil industry. It entrusted administration of the railroads to a

board named by the railroad workers' union. The oil industry was placed in the hands of a government-selected board that included representatives from the oil workers' union. For Trotsky's defense of these nationalizations as anti-imperialist measures, see "Mexico and British Imperialism," in *Writings of Leon Trotsky (1937–38)* (New York: Pathfinder, 1976), pp. 358–61.

6. Soviets, meaning "councils" in Russian, arose in the Russian revolutions of 1905 and 1917 as elected representative bodies of workers, soldiers, and peasants that provided coordination and leadership for their revolutionary struggle. In the fall of 1917 the soviets, with a Bolshevik majority, overthrew the capitalist Provisional Government and established a workers' and peasants' government.

7. A resolution on the united front was adopted at the December 1921 meeting of the Executive Committee of the Communist International. A year later, the resolution on tactics adopted by the November–December 1922 Fourth Congress of the Communist International explained that "the Communists propose to join with all workers belonging to other parties and groups and all unaligned workers in a common struggle to defend the immediate, basic interests of the working class against the bourgeoisie. . . . It is the experience of struggle that will convince workers of the inevitability of revolution and the historic importance of Communism." The resolution cautioned, however, that "any attempt by the Second International to interpret the united front as an organizational fusion of all the 'workers' parties' must of course be categorically repudiated." See *Theses, Resolutions and Manifestos of the First Four Congresses of the Third International* (London: Ink Links, 1980), pp. 395–97 and 400–409.

Pierre Monatte's Syndicalist League engineered a unity pact signed in November 1930 by twenty-two unionists belonging to the CGT and CGTU, and including some unionists outside both these federations. It called for reunification of the labor movement in an organization free of "any interference from political parties." See "Monatte Crosses the Rubicon," in part 2 of this book.

8. Trotsky, "The German Catastrophe: The Responsibility of the Leadership," in *The Struggle against Fascism in Germany* (New York: Pathfinder, 1971), pp. 394–95.

9. British coal miners walked off the job on May 1, 1926. A general strike in their defense began May 4 but was called off on May 12 by the General Council of the Trades Union Congress. The miners' strike ended in defeat six months later.

10. The era of the "rotten boroughs" preceded the British parliamentary reform of 1832, which reapportioned parliamentary seats for the first time since the Middle Ages. Rotten boroughs were electoral districts that had lost almost all of their population, providing an avenue for the wealthy to buy a seat in Parliament.

11. The term *social fascist* was applied by Stalinist forces in the early 1930s to Social Democratic parties and trade unions. Arguing that Social Democrats and fascists were not antagonists but "twins," the Stalinists opposed pressing the Social Democratic organizations for united action to defend the working class from fascism or to achieve other working-class goals.

12. In 1934 the Dutch government forbade municipal workers in Amsterdam from belonging to the NAS.

13. Unemployment benefits were distributed by the Dutch government to jobless workers through their trade union organizations, including the NAS.

14. The automobile magnate Henry Ford (1863–1947), notorious for his brazen antilabor activities, was designated an "economic royalist" by liberals and Stalinists.

15. A "labor party in name only," the American Labor Party, was formed in 1936 in the state of New York. It acted to channel votes of socialist-minded workers to capitalist politicians, placing on its tickets Franklin D. Roosevelt, the Democratic Party presidential candidate, and Fiorello H. La Guardia (1882–1947), Republican Party mayor of New York City.

16. Cannon's article is contained in James P. Cannon, *The Left Opposition in the U.S. 1928–31* (New York: Anchor Foundation, a Pathfinder book, 1981), pp. 315–19.

17. The articles by Cannon are available in Cannon, *The First Ten Years of American Communism* (New York: Pathfinder, 1973), pp. 245–310. Additional material can be found in Farrell Dobbs, *Revolutionary Continuity: The Early Years 1848–1917* (New York: Anchor Foundation, a Pathfinder book, 1980), pp. 97–120, and *Revolutionary Continuity: Birth of the Communist Movement 1918–1922* (New York: Anchor Foundation, a Pathfinder book, 1983), pp. 17–39 and 189–93.

18. The complete record of the Second Congress is available in John Riddell, ed., *Workers and Oppressed Peoples of the World, Unite! Proceedings and Documents of the Second Congress, 1920* (New York: Anchor Foundation, a Pathfinder book, 1990).

19. The story of Liebknecht's revolutionary activity during 1914–19 is told by documents found in Riddell, ed., *Lenin's Struggle for a Revolutionary International* (New York: Anchor Foundation, a Pathfinder book, 1984) and *The German Revolution and the Debate on Soviet Power* (New York: Anchor Foundation, a Pathfinder book, 1986).

20. Revolutionary republics based on workers' and soldiers' councils were established in Hungary and the German state of Bavaria in the spring of 1919, but they were overthrown within a few months. The Russian Soviet Republic faced a civil war from 1918 to 1920 and armed intervention by more than a dozen countries.

21. The Fourth Congress resolutions can be found in Trotsky, *The First Five Years of the Communist International* (New York: Anchor Foundation, a Pathfinder book, 1972), vol. 2, pp. 275–94.

22. The Pact, a secret agreement to exclude Communists from leadership of the French union movement, was signed in February 1921 by eighteen anarchists and syndicalists in preparation for the split in the CGT. The following year the Pact was revealed, and at the June 1922 founding congress of the CGTU, the revolutionary syndicalists close to *La Vie Ouvrière*, backed by the Communists, gained a majority.

23. In a December 15, 1922, article in *La Vie Ouvrière*, "The Return to Marx and the Adherence [of the CGTU] to the RILU," Louzon wrote:
"'Unconsciously to themselves,' said Marx, 'the trades' unions were

forming centers of organization of the working class, as the medieval municipalities and communes did for the middle class.' '[The unions represent] organized agencies for superseding the very system of wages labor and capital rule.' 'Only the unions can form the real workers' party.'

"This is the goal, this is the mission that Marx assigned to the unions.

"But what is the essential condition for the unions to be able to accomplish this mission?

"Again, let us allow Marx to speak.

"'The unions, if they are to fulfill their mission, should not serve as an appendage to *any political party*.' 'If the unions do not remain independent of political parties, *that's the end of them*.'"

The first two sentences of Louzon's quote are from Marx's article, "Trade Unions: Their Past, Present, and Future," which is included as the prologue to this book. The sentence: "Only the unions can form the real workers' party," as well as Louzon's other citations in the final paragraph are taken not from Marx's writings but from the account of a discussion with him by J. Hamann, a German trade union leader. For Hamann's account see Hal Draper, *Karl Marx's Theory of Revolution*, vol. 2 (New York: Monthly Review, 1978), pp. 585–87.

24. The reference to the German workers' organizations as "nothing more than a left wing of the democratic party" applies to the mid-1800s, the period of struggle to unify Germany and complete the bourgeois revolution. Eisenach is the German city where the Social Democratic Workers Party was founded in 1869 by supporters of Marx. A rival organization, the General Union of German Workers, was led by followers of Ferdinand Lassalle. Lassalleans and Eisenachers united in the Social Democratic Workers Party at an 1875 congress in Gotha.

25. "Yellow confederation" refers to the CGT. Originally a reference to French company unions formed in the late 1800s, which had a yellow flower for their insignia, the term *Yellow* was soon applied more generally to labor organizations with proemployer or traitorous leaderships.

26. The "centrist bureaucracy" referred to here is the Stalinist leadership of the Communist International, which justified its ultraleft policies by claims of imminent revolution. At the September 1929 CGTU congress, Syndicalist League leader Maurice Chambelland had

counterposed to this the prediction that capitalism would experience peaceful development for another thirty or forty years.

Trotsky referred to the Stalinist bureaucracy as "bureaucratic centrist" in the early 1930s to underline its tendency to waver between revolutionary and reformist policies. After about 1935, he no longer used the term. Stalinism had now become the "crudest form of opportunism and social patriotism," Trotsky wrote in 1937. *Writings of Leon Trotsky (1933–34)* (New York: Pathfinder, 1975), p. 340.

27. Jules Guesde (1845–1922), a leader of the wing of the French working-class movement that looked to Marxism and a founder of the Socialist Party, took a chauvinist stand in 1914 in support of World War I and became a French government minister.

28. See "A Necessary Discussion with Our Syndicalist Comrades," found earlier in this collection.

29. "Bolshevization" of the Comintern parties was a central theme of its Fifth Congress, held in 1924. This effort, headed by Comintern chairman Gregory Zinoviev, imposed on member parties bureaucratic practices that had gained the upper hand in the Soviet party after V.I. Lenin was forced to withdraw from political activity early in 1923. Bolshevization provided a banner under which the campaign led by Stalin and Zinoviev against Trotsky and the Left Opposition was extended from the Soviet party to the entire International.

Quai de Jemmapes was the street where the offices of Monatte's newspaper *La Vie Ouvrière* were located.

30. Lenin's "testament" is a letter to the Twelfth Congress of the Russian Communist Party, which he dictated in late December 1922 and early January 1923. The letter proposed measures to strengthen the party's proletarian character and combat the process of growing bureaucratization expressed and promoted above all by Stalin. The letter was suppressed by Stalin and his supporters, who denied its existence until 1956. It is printed in V.I. Lenin, *Collected Works*, vol. 36 (Moscow: Progress Publishers, 1966), pp. 593–611.

31. In January 1915 Sébastien Faure (1858–1942) issued an appeal calling for struggle against World War I. It was widely circulated, including

among French soldiers. When French Interior Minister Louis Malvy (1875–1949) threatened to prosecute soldiers with whom Faure was in contact, Faure made a deal with Malvy renouncing antiwar agitation.

32. Chambelland had written a letter earlier in 1930 claiming that the Left Opposition was a centrist force vacillating between syndicalist forces favoring trade union autonomy and the CGTU leadership. Trotsky's answer, "What is Centrism?" is found in *Writings of Leon Trotsky (1930)* (New York: Pathfinder, 1975), pp. 234–41.

33. An uprising in February 1930 against the French colonial administration in Indochina was met with mass arrests and bombings of villages. Thirteen leaders of the Vietnamese nationalist movement were executed by French authorities on June 17, 1930.

34. In March 1930, Mohandas Gandhi, leader of India's struggle for independence from British colonial rule, had launched a massive civil disobedience campaign against the tax on salt levied by the British authorities. The Labour Party government of Prime Minister James Ramsey MacDonald responded with force, jailing more than sixty thousand people. James H. Thomas, general secretary of the railworkers' union, was a prominent member of MacDonald's cabinet.

George Nathaniel Curzon (1859–1925) was the British viceroy of India from 1899 to 1905 and British foreign secretary from 1919 to 1924.

35. The Treaty of Versailles, imposed on Germany following World War I, exacted enormous war reparations. In 1929 right-wing parties in Germany seized on negotiations over further payments to whip up nationalist sentiment. In the September 1930 elections the Nazi party increased its vote six times over and gained nearly one hundred seats in the German parliament. The day the new parliament convened, anti-Semitic riots were organized in Berlin.

36. Stalin's theory of a "two-class workers' and peasants' party," first advanced in 1924, called for the formation in backward countries of "a revolutionary bloc between the workers and the petty bourgeoisie" in the form of "a single party, a workers' and peasants' party, akin to the Kuomintang." Quoting this statement, Trotsky commented in 1928 that

Stalin's theory "seems to have been specially created to camouflage bourgeois parties" like the Kuomintang, which seek support from the peasant and worker masses. See Trotsky, *The Third International after Lenin* (New York: Pathfinder, 1970), pp. 214, 216. For a recent presentation of communist policy in forging an alliance of workers and exploited farmers and for the relationship of this alliance to building a communist party, see Jack Barnes, "The Fight for a Workers' and Farmers' Government in the United States," in *New International*, no. 4 (Spring 1985).

37. In 1927 the Kuomintang carried out a brutal massacre of the revolutionary working class in Shanghai and other centers, dealing a decisive blow to the revolutionary upsurge that had begun two years earlier. For Trotsky's views on the Chinese revolution, see *Leon Trotsky on China* (New York: Anchor Foundation, a Pathfinder book, 1976).

38. The "strikebreakers" were the leaders of the British Trades Union Congress, who betrayed the miners and the general strike in May 1926. Two months later, at a meeting of the Russian Communist Party Central Committee, five Central Committee members submitted a resolution drafted by Trotsky demanding that Soviet trade union leaders withdraw from the Anglo-Russian Trade Union Unity Committee. This resolution and other material on the 1926 general strike are found in *Leon Trotsky on Britain* (New York: Anchor Foundation, a Pathfinder book, 1973).

39. The POP, or Workers and Peasants Party, was formed at the end of 1929 by Louis Sellier and others expelled from the French Communist Party as part of the purge of supporters of Nikolai Bukharin. Monatte's current, which led the Committee for Trade Union Independence, operated in the CGTU in a bloc with members of the Workers and Peasants Party.

Glossary

Allies – the victorious powers in World War I, headed by Britain, France, and the United States.

American Federation of Labor (AFL) – founded 1881; U.S. labor federation based on skilled craft unions; Committee for Industrial Organization affiliates were driven out in 1936 and formed separate CIO federation; AFL and CIO merged 1955.

Amsterdam International (International Federation of Trade Unions) – founded July 1919 in Amsterdam by Social Democratic trade union officials; claimed 24 million members in 1920.

Anglo-Russian Trade Union Unity Committee – founded May 1925 by leaderships of British and Soviet trade unions; dissolved September 1927 when British members walked out.

Bakunin, Mikhail (1814–1876) – leader and theorist of anarchist movement; combated views of Marx and Engels within International Working Men's Association.

Blum, Léon (1872–1950) – French SP leader after 1921 split that formed CP.

Bolshevik-Leninists – see International Left Opposition.

Bolshevik Party – originated in 1903 as majority faction of Russian Social Democratic Labor Party; led October 1917 Russian revolution; took name Communist Party of Russia (Bolsheviks) in 1918.

Brandlerites (Brandler group) – formed early 1929 as Communist Party of Germany (Opposition) by supporters of Heinrich Brandler (1881–1967) and other leaders of German Communist Party who had been expelled for supporting Right Opposition in Russian CP.

Bukharin, Nikolai (1888–1938) – a central leader of Bolshevik Party and Communist International; allied with Stalin 1923–28; headed Right Opposition to Stalin and was expelled from party

1929; later recanted and was readmitted; executed after third Moscow frame-up trial.

Cachin, Marcel (1869–1958) – leader of French SP during World War I; supported government war policy until 1917; helped lead French SP majority into Communist International 1920; as leader of CP, was aligned with Stalin from mid-1920s.

Cannon, James P. (1890–1974) – U.S. communist leader; originally IWW organizer and leader of SP left wing; founder of CP 1919; expelled from CP for supporting Left Opposition 1928; founding leader of International Left Opposition and U.S. Socialist Workers Party.

CGT – see General Confederation of Labor.

CGTU – see Unitary General Confederation of Labor.

Chambelland, Maurice (1901–1966) – member of *La Vie Ouvrière* group in early 1920s; joined French CP 1923; expelled 1924; founding secretary of Syndicalist League 1926; close associate of Pierre Monatte.

Charter of Amiens – syndicalist resolution adopted by CGT at 1906 congress in Amiens; declared CGT's independence from all political parties.

CIO – see Congress of Industrial Organizations.

Citrine, Walter (1887–1983) – general secretary of British Trades Union Congress 1926–46.

Clynes, John R. (1869–1949) – president of General and Municipal Workers' Union 1914–37; member of British Labour Party National Executive Committee 1909–39; member of World War I coalition government.

Committee for Trade Union Independence – syndicalist opposition in CGTU initiated in early 1930 by supporters of Syndicalist League; based in unions of dockworkers, food workers, and printers.

Communist International (Comintern, Third International) – founded on initiative of Russian CP in 1919 as worldwide party of socialist revolution; dominated after Lenin's death by Stalin and other representatives of ruling conservative bureaucratic caste in Soviet Union; dissolved 1943.

Communist League (France) – Left Opposition group in France formed

April 1930; published newspaper *La Vérité*.

Communist League of America – U.S. Left Opposition group founded May 1929; predecessor of Socialist Workers Party.

Communist Party of France – formed December 1920 by majority of French Socialist Party; right-wing minority split, retaining name Socialist Party.

Congress of Industrial Organizations (CIO) – U.S. industrial union federation formed in 1935 as Committee for Industrial Organization inside American Federation of Labor; suspended from AFL 1936 and formed separate federation; expelled 1938; merged with AFL to form AFL-CIO 1955.

Conservative Party – main party of British bourgeoisie after World War I.

Cook, Arthur J. (1883–1931) – British trade union leader; elected secretary of Miners Federation of Great Britain in 1924 with support of Minority Movement; member of Anglo-Russian Trade Union Unity Committee; became member of Trades Union Congress General Council 1927.

Debs, Eugene V. (1855–1926) – spokesman for U.S. SP and five-time presidential candidate; imprisoned for antiwar statements 1918–21; solidarized with Russian revolution but remained in SP following 1919 split that formed Communist Party.

Dumoulin, Georges (1877–1963) – French unionist; a leader of opposition in CGT to World War I; went over to Jouhaux and right wing 1918; CGT administrative secretary following 1921 split; initiator with Monatte of December 1930 statement for CGT-CGTU unity.

Epigones – "inferior imitators"; term often used by Trotsky to refer to Stalinists, who corrupt and distort the ideas of Marx and Lenin.

Fourth International – world revolutionary party formed in 1938 by forces seeking to rebuild international communist movement; its most prominent leader was Leon Trotsky.

Freemasons – secret society originating in medieval stonemasons' guilds; in France and Italy especially, it espoused democratic ideas and admitted Socialists as well as bourgeois professionals; defender of bourgeois order.

Frossard, Louis-Oscar (1889–1946) – centrist French SP leader during World War I; general secretary of SP 1918–20 and of CP 1920–23; broke with CP 1923 and later rejoined SP.

General Confederation of Labor (CGT) – founded 1895; at 1906 congress in Amiens adopted syndicalist stands, declaring itself independent from all political parties; majority leadership supported French government in World War I; left-wing minority was expelled and formed CGTU in June 1922; although claiming to maintain syndicalist position, CGT became identified with French Socialist Party; CGTU and CGT reunited as CGT in 1936.

Hague, Frank P. (1876–1956) – Democratic Party mayor of Jersey City, New Jersey 1917–47; during 1930s gained national notoriety for use of police in cooperation with company thugs to try to drive labor organizers out of city.

Henderson, Arthur (1863–1935) – British Labour Party general secretary 1911–34.

Hicks, George (1879–1954) – British trade union official; headed General Council of Trades Union Congress 1926–27.

Independent Labour Party (ILP) – founded 1893; affiliated to Second International and British Labour Party; left wing joined in formation of British CP 1921; broke with Labour Party and Second International in 1932 and was a sponsor of 1933 Paris conference to discuss new revolutionary International; rejoined Labour Party in 1939.

Industrial Workers of the World (IWW) – founded in U.S. 1905; adopted syndicalist positions, rejecting political action and work in American Federation of Labor; opposed U.S. participation in World War I and suffered severe repression; went into decline after 1919 formation of CP; rejected affiliation to Red International of Labor Unions 1921.

International Left Opposition – organized 1930 by Leon Trotsky and others to defend communist perspective in Comintern against deepening Stalinist degeneration; continuator of Left Opposition organized by Trotsky and others in Soviet CP 1923; became International Communist League 1933, Movement for the Fourth

International 1936; established Fourth International 1938.

International Working Men's Association (First International) – founded 1864; led by Marx and Engels; united working-class organizations in Europe and North America; participated in 1871 Paris Commune and its international defense; following defeat of Paris Commune, headquarters moved from London to New York 1872; disbanded 1876.

Jouhaux, Léon (1879–1954) – head of French CGT 1909–40, 1945–47; leader of Amsterdam International Federation of Trade Unions.

Kornilov, Lavr G. (1870–1918) – tsarist general; commander in chief under 1917 Provisional Government; led attempted right-wing putsch August 1917; led counterrevolutionary armies after October revolution.

Kuomintang (Nationalist Party) – Chinese bourgeois-nationalist party founded 1912; conducted struggle for national unity and bourgeois reform; Chinese CP members joined 1923; admitted as sympathizing party to Comintern 1926; organized massacre of working class 1927; overthrown by 1949 revolution.

Labour Party (Britain) – founded 1906 as federation of trade unions and affiliated social democratic organizations.

Lassalle, Ferdinand (1825–1864) – German socialist leader and organizer of General Union of German Workers 1863; criticized by Marx for opportunist positions and concessions to Prussian state.

League of the Rights of Man – French bourgeois organization formed 1898 to defend democratic rights.

Left Opposition – see International Left Opposition.

Lenin, Vladimir Ilyich (1870–1924) – a founder of Russian Social Democratic Labor Party and central leader of Bolsheviks from 1903; chair of Council of People's Commissars (Russian Soviet government) 1917–24; central leader of Comintern.

Lewis, John L. (1880–1969) – president of United Mine Workers of America 1919–60; president of CIO 1935–40.

Liberal Party – major party of British bourgeoisie before World War I; declined after war in face of rise of Labour Party.

Liebknecht, Karl (1871–1919) – only Social Democratic Party member of German parliament to vote in 1914 against money for

World War I; imprisoned for May 1, 1916, antiwar speech in Potsdam Square; a founding leader of German Communist Party; arrested and murdered January 1919.

Longuet, Jean (1876–1938) – leader of French SP's centrist wing; criticized SP's all-out support to government war policy during World War I but voted for war spending; opposed Communist International; went with right-wing minority in 1920 split.

Loriot, Fernand (1870–1932) – leader of revolutionary left in French SP during and after World War I; French CP international secretary 1921; opposed bureaucratization of CP and quit party 1926; worked with Left Opposition currents and joined Syndicalist League.

Louzon, Robert (1882–1976) – syndicalist and collaborator of Monatte; resigned from French CP 1924 to help found *La Révolution Prolétarienne;* active in Syndicalist League.

Lovestoneites – Right Opposition group in U.S.; founded by Jay Lovestone (1898–1990), CP general secretary who was expelled as supporter of Right Opposition 1929.

Lozovsky, Solomon A. (1878–1952) – member of Russian Communist Party; general secretary of Red International of Labor Unions 1921–37; supported Stalin from mid-1920s; arrested 1949 and shot in prison.

MacDonald, James Ramsey (1866–1937) – British Labour Party prime minister 1924, 1929–31; split from Labour Party to form coalition government in 1931.

Manuilsky, Dmitri Z. (1883–1959) – member of Russian Communist Party; key ideologist of Stalinism in 1920s; headed Comintern 1929–34; a leading theorist of ultraleft "third period" turn 1928–34.

Menshevik Party – originated in 1903 as reformist wing of Russian Social Democratic Labor Party; opposed October 1917 Russian revolution.

Merrheim, Alphonse (1871–1925) – secretary of French metalworkers' union after 1905; a leader of opposition in CGT to World War I; went over to Jouhaux and right wing 1918; remained with CGT after 1921 split.

Minority Movement – left-wing caucus in British Trades Union Congress initiated by Communist Party in 1924.

Monatte, Pierre (1881–1960) – French syndicalist; founded *La Vie Ouvrière* 1909; resigned in 1915 from CGT National Council to protest its support to World War I; joined French CP 1923; opposed anti-Trotsky campaign and was expelled 1924; returned to syndicalist positions, founding *La Révolution Prolétarienne* and Syndicalist League.

Monmousseau, Gaston (1883–1960) – French syndicalist; secretary of railworkers' union April 1920; a CGTU leader from June 1922 founding congress; joined French CP 1925.

Mosley, Sir Oswald (1896–1980) – headed British Union of Fascists during 1930s.

National Labor Secretariat (NAS) – founded 1893; during 1930s was small left-wing rival to major Dutch labor federation, organizing construction workers and dockworkers, as well as Amsterdam municipal workers prior to 1934.

New Left – political current in student and youth radicalization of 1960s that rejected Stalinism and social democracy as conservative ideologies; also rejected Leninism and the working class as agent of social change.

Profintern – see Red International of Labor Unions.

Proudhon, Pierre-Joseph (1809–1865) – utopian socialist; put forward ideas of a society based on fair exchange between producers and replacement of the state by a network of workshops; influenced French anarchism and syndicalism.

Purcell, Albert A. (1872–1935) – British trade union leader; member of Trades Union Congress General Council 1919–27 and of Anglo-Russian Trade Union Unity Committee.

Red International of Labor Unions (RILU, Profintern) – founded July 1921 in Moscow by trade union forces in Comintern, syndicalist unions, and left-wing forces in Amsterdam trade union International.

Renaudel, Pierre (1871–1935) – central leader of French SP during World War I and leader of its right wing; went with right-wing minority split that retained SP name 1920.

Revolutionary Socialist Workers Party (RSAP) – founded 1934–35 from fusion of Dutch revolutionary groups; led by Henk Sneevliet; affiliated to Left Opposition but broke with it prior to 1938 founding of Fourth International.

La Révolution Prolétarienne – newspaper founded 1925 by Pierre Monatte, Alfred Rosmer, and others opposed to CP policies; initially sympathetic to Left Opposition; defined itself as "Communist-Syndicalist."

Right Opposition – current led by Bukharin in Soviet CP and Comintern that opposed Stalin 1928–29; supporters were expelled from Comintern, forming International Communist Opposition in 1930; see Lovestoneites, Brandlerites.

Roosevelt, Franklin D. (1882–1945) – Democratic Party president of U.S. 1933–45; supported as a progressive by Stalinists, social democrats, and most officials in AFL and CIO.

Rosmer, Alfred (1877–1964) – French syndicalist; internationalist opponent of CGT leadership during World War I; founding member of French CP; expelled from CP 1924 as supporter of Left Opposition and helped found *La Révolution Prolétarienne;* broke with Left Opposition 1930; renewed collaboration with Trotsky 1936.

Second International (Socialist International, Social Democracy) – founded 1889 as international association of workers' parties; collapsed at outbreak of World War I when majority of leaders supported their own governments; revolutionary left wing founded Communist International 1919; right wing formed Labor and Socialist International 1923.

Sellier, Louis (1885–1978) – French CP general secretary 1923–24; expelled with five other CP Paris municipal councillors November 1929 for supporting Right Opposition; helped found Workers and Peasants Party (POP) December 1929.

Sémard, Pierre (1887–1942) – syndicalist and French SP member during World War I; CP general secretary 1924–29.

Sembat, Marcel (1862–1922) – prominent right-wing French SP leader; government minister 1914–16.

Sneevliet, Henk (1883–1942) – trade union organizer in the Netherlands and Dutch East Indies (Indonesia); Comintern leader from 1920; quit CP 1927; founded Revolutionary Socialist Party 1929, Revolutionary Socialist Workers Party (RSAP), 1934–35; elected to parliament 1933; cosigned call with Trotsky for new International 1933 but broke with Fourth International movement before 1938; executed by Nazi troops during German occupation.

Social Democracy – after 1917, refers to parties of reformist Second International, which opposed Bolshevik-led revolution in Russia and opposed Comintern.

Socialist Party of France – founded by merger of two Socialist parties 1905; majority leadership supported French government in World War I; centrist minority won leadership in July 1918; joined Communist International December 1920 and changed name to Communist Party; minority (Dissidents) split and reestablished Socialist Party.

Socialist Revolutionary Party (SRs) – Russian petty-bourgeois party founded 1900; had strong base in peasantry; right wing opposed October 1917 revolution; left wing initially supported it but later went over to counterrevolution.

Stalin, Joseph (1879–1953) – a leader of Bolshevik Party; presided over bureaucratic degeneration of Russian CP and Comintern and their rejection of revolutionary internationalist course; organized frame-up trials in 1930s and liquidation of majority of Bolshevik leaders of Lenin's time.

Syndicalist League – founded in 1926 by Pierre Monatte, Maurice Chambelland, and others as trade union opposition working to reunify CGT and CGTU on syndicalist basis.

Le Temps – leading French newspaper between world wars; regarded as semiofficial voice of government.

Third International – see Communist International.

Thomas, James H. (1874–1949) – British trade union official and cabinet member in 1924 and 1929–31 Labour Party governments; split from Labour Party with MacDonald to form coalition government 1931.

Trades Union Congress – British trade union federation founded in 1868.

Unitary General Confederation of Labor (CGTU) – founding congress held June 1922 after split in CGT, with supporters of Communist Party in majority; affiliated to Red International of Labor Unions late 1922; reunified with CGT in 1936.

Unitary Opposition – left-wing grouping in CGTU formed April 1930 by leaders of CGTU Teachers Federation, supported by Communist League trade unionists.

Varenne, Alexandre (1870–1947) – member of French parliament 1906–10, 1914–36; part of SP pro-war majority during World War I; when French CP formed, split along with right wing to reestablish SP 1920.

Vassart, Albert (1898–1958) – syndicalist; joined French CP 1921; leader of CGTU and CP.

Verfeuil, Raoul (1887–1927) – French centrist SP leader; stayed with majority that formed CP 1920; expelled at October 1922 CP congress.

La Vérité – French Left Opposition weekly, 1929–36.

La Vie Ouvrière – newspaper founded by Pierre Monatte in 1909; voice of syndicalists who supported Comintern during early 1920s.

Zinoviev, Gregory (1883–1936) – a central leader of Bolshevik Party; chairman of Comintern 1919–26; aligned with Stalin 1923–25; joined Trotsky 1926–27 in United Opposition; capitulated 1928; convicted at first Moscow frame-up trial and executed.

Zyromsky, Jean (1890–1975) – leader during 1930s of left wing in French SP; advocated "organic unity" with CP; joined CP 1945.

Index

THE TEAMSTER SERIES

LESSONS FROM THE LABOR BATTLES OF THE 1930S
BY FARRELL DOBBS

Teamster Rebellion

The 1934 strikes that built the industrial union movement in Minneapolis and helped pave the way for the CIO, recounted by a central leader of that battle. The first in a four-volume series. The subsequent volumes describe . . .

Teamster Power

. . . how the class-struggle Teamsters leadership used the power workers had won during the 1934 strikes to make Minneapolis a union town and launch an 11-state campaign that brought tens of thousands of over-the-road truckers into the union . . .

Teamster Politics

. . . how they combated FBI frame-ups, helped the jobless organize, deployed a Union Defense Guard to turn back fascist thugs, fought to advance independent labor political action, and mobilized opposition to U.S. imperialism's entry into World War II . . .

Teamster Bureaucracy

. . . how the employing class, backed by union bureaucrats, stepped up government efforts to gag class-conscious militants, and how workers mounted a world campaign to free eighteen union and socialist leaders framed up and imprisoned in the infamous 1941 federal sedition trial.

Each volume $19

Unions Their past, present, and future

The Eastern Airlines Strike
ACCOMPLISHMENTS OF THE
RANK-AND-FILE MACHINISTS
*Ernie Mailhot, Judy Stranahan,
and Jack Barnes*
The story of the 686-day strike in which a
rank-and-file resistance by Machinists
prevented Eastern's union-busting
onslaught from becoming the road toward
a profitable nonunion airline. $9.95

The 1985–86 Hormel Meat-Packers Strike in Austin, Minnesota
Fred Halstead

The hard-fought strike against Hormel opened a round of battles
by packinghouse workers that—together with strikes by paper
workers, cannery workers, and western coal miners—marked a
break in the rout of U.S. unions that began during the 1981–82
recession. $5

The Transitional Program for Socialist Revolution
Leon Trotsky

Contains discussions between leaders of the U.S. Socialist
Workers Party and exiled revolutionary Leon Trotsky in 1938.
The product of these discussions, a program of immediate,
democratic, and transitional demands, was adopted by the SWP
later that year. This program for socialist revolution remains an
irreplaceable component of a fighting guide for communist
workers today. $23.95

Labor's Giant Step
THE FIRST TWENTY YEARS OF THE CIO: 1936–55
Art Preis

The story of the explosive labor struggles and political battles in
the 1930s that built the industrial unions. And how those unions
became the vanguard of a mass social movement that began
transforming U.S. society. $30

Order from www.pathfinderpress.com

THE CUBAN REVOLUTION

Episodes of the Cuban Revolutionary War, 1956–58

ERNESTO CHE GUEVARA

A firsthand account of the political events and military campaigns that culminated in the January 1959 popular insurrection that overthrew the U.S.-backed dictatorship in Cuba. With clarity and humor, Guevara describes his own political education. He explains how the struggle transformed the men and women of the Rebel Army and July 26 Movement, opening the door to the first socialist revolution in the Americas. $23.95 Also in Spanish.

Cuba and the Coming American Revolution

JACK BARNES

"There will be a victorious revolution in the United States before there will be a victorious counterrevolution in Cuba." That statement, made by Fidel Castro in 1961, remains as accurate today as when it was spoken. This is a book about the class struggle in the United States, where the revolutionary capacities of workers and farmers are today as utterly discounted by the ruling powers as were those of the Cuban toilers. And just as wrongly. $13 Also in Spanish and French.

www.pathfinderpress.com

Aldabonazo
Inside the Cuban Revolutionary Underground, 1952–58
ARMANDO HART

In this firsthand account by a historic leader of the Cuban Revolution, we meet men and women who led the urban underground in the fight against the brutal U.S.-backed tyranny in the 1950s. Together with their comrades-in-arms in the Rebel Army, they not only overthrew the dictatorship. Their revolutionary actions and example worldwide changed the history of the 20th century—and the century to come. $25

Making History
Interviews with Four Generals of Cuba's Revolutionary Armed Forces
Through the stories of four outstanding Cuban generals—Néstor López Cuba, Enrique Carreras, José Ramón Fernández, and Harry Villegas—each with close to half a century of revolutionary activity, we can see the class dynamics that shaped the Cuban Revolution and our entire epoch. $15.95 Also in Spanish.

From the Escambray to the Congo
In the Whirlwind of the Cuban Revolution
VÍCTOR DREKE

In this participant's account, Víctor Dreke describes how easy it became after the Cuban Revolution to take down a rope segregating blacks from whites at a dance in the town square, yet how enormous was the battle to transform social relations underlying all the "ropes" inherited from capitalism and Yankee domination. $17 Also in Spanish.

Dynamics of the Cuban Revolution
A Marxist Appreciation
JOSEPH HANSEN
How did the Cuban Revolution come about? Why does it represent, as Hansen puts it, an "unbearable challenge" to U.S. imperialism? What political obstacles has it overcome? Written as the revolution advanced from its earliest days. $22.95

www.pathfinderpress.com

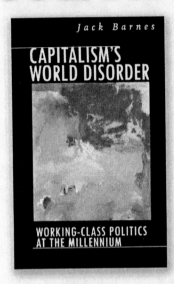

Jack Barnes

CAPITALISM'S WORLD DISORDER

WORKING-CLASS POLITICS AT THE MILLENNIUM

Capitalism's World Disorder
Working-Class Politics at the Millennium
JACK BARNES

The social devastation and financial panic, the coarsening of politics, the cop brutality and acts of imperialist aggression accelerating around us—all are the product not of something gone wrong with capitalism but of its lawful workings. Yet the future can be changed by the united struggle and selfless action of workers and farmers conscious of their power to transform the world. $23.95 Also in Spanish and French.

The Long View of History
GEORGE NOVACK

Revolutionary change is fundamental to social and cultural progress. This pamphlet explains why—and how the struggle by working people to end oppression and exploitation is a realistic perspective built on sound scientific foundations. $7

The Struggle for a Proletarian Party
JAMES P. CANNON

"The workers of America have power enough to topple the structure of capitalism at home and to lift the whole world with them when they rise," Cannon asserts. On the eve of World War II, a founder of the communist movement in the U.S. and leader of the Communist International in Lenin's time defends the program and party-building norms of Bolshevism. $21.95

COSMETICS FASHIONS AND THE EXPLOITATION OF WOMEN

JOSEPH HANSEN
EVELYN REED
MARY-ALICE WATERS

Cosmetics, Fashions, and the Exploitation of Women
JOSEPH HANSEN, EVELYN REED, MARY-ALICE WATERS

How big business plays on women's second-class status and social insecurities to market cosmetics and rake in profits. The introduction by Waters explains how the entry of millions of women into the workforce during and after World War II irreversibly changed U.S. society and laid the basis for a renewed rise of struggles for women's emancipation. $14.95

www.pathfinderpress.com

To Speak the Truth
Why Washington's 'Cold War' against Cuba Doesn't End
FIDEL CASTRO, ERNESTO CHE GUEVARA

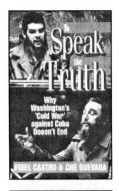

"In the coming year, our country intends to wage its great battle against illiteracy, with the ambitious goal of teaching every single illiterate person to read and write," Fidel Castro told the UN General Assembly in September 1960. A year later that task was done. In speeches before UN assemblies, two leaders of Cuba's socialist revolution present its political gains and internationalist course. They explain why Washington so hates Cuba's example and why its effort to destroy the revolution will fail. $16.95

Malcolm X Talks to Young People

Four talks and an interview given to young people in Ghana, the United Kingdom, and the United States in the last months of Malcolm's life. This new edition contains the entire December 1964 presentation by Malcolm X at the Oxford Union in the United Kingdom, in print for the first time anywhere. The collection concludes with two memorial tributes by a young socialist leader to this great revolutionary. With a new preface and an expanded photo display of 17 pages. $15

The Jewish Question
A Marxist Interpretation
ABRAM LEON

Traces the historical rationalizations of anti-Semitism to the fact that Jews—in the centuries preceding the domination of industrial capitalism—emerged as a "people-class" of merchants and moneylenders. Leon explains why the propertied rulers incite renewed Jew-hatred in the epoch of capitalism's decline. $17.95

John Coltrane and the Jazz Revolution of the 1960s
FRANK KOFSKY

An account of John Coltrane's role in spearheading innovations in jazz that were an expression of the new cultural and political ferment that marked the rise of the mass struggle for Black rights. $23.95

"Without revolutionary theory,

FROM THE PAGES OF 'NEW INTERNATIONAL'

Each issue of this magazine of Marxist politics and theory features articles by leaders of the communist movement analyzing today's world of capitalist economic crisis, sharpening interimperialist conflict, and accelerated drive toward war. Among the questions of revolutionary working-class strategy discussed in its pages are . . .

U.S. IMPERIALISM HAS LOST THE COLD WAR
by Jack Barnes

Contrary to imperialist expectations in the wake of the collapse of regimes across Eastern Europe and the USSR claiming to be communist, the working class there has not been crushed. It remains an intractable obstacle to stabilizing capitalist relations, one the exploiters will have to confront in class battles and war. In *New International* no. 11. $14 Also in Spanish, French, and Swedish.

OPENING GUNS OF WORLD WAR III: WASHINGTON'S ASSAULT ON IRAQ
by Jack Barnes

"Washington's slaughter in the Gulf in 1991 is the first in a number of conflicts and wars that will be initiated by the U.S. rulers in the 1990s. . . . Never has the gap been greater in the Middle East between toilers' aspirations for national sovereignty, democracy, and social justice and the political course of bourgeois misleaderships. That fact marks the dead end of advancing these goals today in the name of 'pan-Arab' or 'pan-Islamic' unity." In *New International* no. 7. $12 Also in Spanish, French, and Swedish.

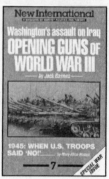

there can be no revolutionary movement."
— V.I. LENIN

DEFENDING CUBA, DEFENDING CUBA'S SOCIALIST REVOLUTION

by Mary-Alice Waters

"As working people enter into struggle with the employing class and its political representatives in Washington, the most combative and class-conscious workers will increasingly understand the stakes in standing shoulder to shoulder with the working class in Cuba, which is fighting in similar trenches against a common class enemy." In *New International* no. 10. $14 Also in Spanish, French, and Swedish.

THE RISE AND FALL OF THE NICARAGUAN REVOLUTION

by Jack Barnes, Steve Clark, and Larry Seigle

Recounts the achievements and worldwide impact of the 1979 Nicaraguan revolution and traces the political retreat of the Sandinista National Liberation Front leadership that led to the downfall of the workers and farmers government in the closing years of the 1980s. In *New International* no. 9. $16 Also in Spanish.

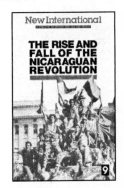

WASHINGTON'S 50-YEAR DOMESTIC CONTRA OPERATION

by Larry Seigle

As the U.S. rulers prepared to smash working-class resistance and join the interimperialist slaughter of World War II, the federal political police apparatus as it exists today was born, together with vastly expanded executive powers of the imperial presidency. This article describes the consequences for the labor, Black, antiwar, and other social movements and how communists have fought over the past fifty years to defend workers rights against government and employer attacks. In *New International* no. 6. $15 Available in Spanish as booklet. $7

www.pathfinderpress.com

FROM THE ARSENAL OF MARXISM

The Communist Manifesto

Karl Marx, Frederick Engels
Founding document of the modern
working-class movement, published in
1848. Explains why communism is
derived not from preconceived
principles but from *facts* and from
proletarian movements that are the
product of the workings of capitalism
itself. $3.95
Also in Spanish and French.

Socialism: Utopian and Scientific

Frederick Engels
"The task of scientific socialism," wrote Frederick Engels in 1877, is "to
impart to the now oppressed proletarian class a full knowledge of the
momentous [revolution] it is called upon to accomplish." $4

Lenin's Final Fight

SPEECHES AND WRITINGS, 1922–23
V.I. Lenin
In the early 1920s Lenin waged a political battle in
the Communist Party leadership in the USSR to
maintain the course that had enabled workers and
peasants to overthrow the tsarist empire, carry out
the first socialist revolution, and begin building a
world communist movement. The issues posed in
this fight—from the leadership's class
composition, to the worker-peasant alliance and
battle against national oppression—remain
central to world politics today. $19.95
Also in Spanish.

www.pathfinderpress.com